I0008641

Transformative Artificial Intelligence (AI) Driverless Self-Driving Cars

Practical Advances in Artificial Intelligence (AI) and Machine Learning

Dr. Lance B. Eliot, MBA, PhD

Disclaimer: This book is presented solely for educational and entertainment purposes. The author and publisher are not offering it as legal, accounting, or other professional services advice. The author and publisher make no representations or warranties of any kind and assume no liabilities of any kind with respect to the accuracy or completeness of the contents and specifically disclaim any implied warranties of merchantability or fitness of use for a particular purpose. Neither the author nor the publisher shall be held liable or responsible to any person or entity with respect to any loss or incidental or consequential damages caused, or alleged to have been caused, directly or indirectly, by the information or programs contained herein. Every company is different and the advice and strategies contained herein may not be suitable for your situation.

DEDICATION

To my incredible son, Michael and my incredible daughter, Lauren.

Forest fortuna adiuvat (from the Latin; good fortune favors the brave).

CONTENTS

Lance B. Eliot

ACKNOWLEDGMENTS

I have been the beneficiary of advice and counsel by many friends, colleagues, family, investors, and many others. I want to thank everyone that has aided me throughout my career. I write from the heart and the head, having experienced first-hand what it means to have others around you that support you during the good times and the tough times.

To Warren Bennis, one of my doctoral advisors and ultimately a colleague, I offer my deepest thanks and appreciation, especially for his calm and insightful wisdom and support.

To Mark Stevens and his generous efforts toward funding and supporting the USC Stevens Center for Innovation.

To Lloyd Greif and the USC Lloyd Greif Center for Entrepreneurial Studies for their ongoing encouragement of founders and entrepreneurs.

To Peter Drucker, William Wang, Aaron Levie, Peter Kim, Jon Kraft, Cindy Crawford, Jenny Ming, Steve Milligan, Chis Underwood, Frank Gehry, Buzz Aldrin, Steve Forbes, Bill Thompson, Dave Dillon, Alan Fuerstman, Larry Ellison, Jim Sinegal, John Sperling, Mark Stevenson, Anand Nallathambi, Thomas Barrack, Jr., and many other innovators and leaders that I have met and gained mightily from doing so.

Thanks to Ed Trainor, Kevin Anderson, James Hickey, Wendell Jones, Ken Harris, DuWayne Peterson, Mike Brown, Jim Thornton, Abhi Beniwal, Al Biland, John Nomura, Eliot Weinman, John Desmond, and many others for their unwavering support during my career.

And most of all thanks as always to Lauren and Michael, for their ongoing support and for having seen me writing and heard much of this material during the many months involved in writing it. To their patience and willingness to listen.

Lance B. Eliot

INTRODUCTION

This is a book that provides the newest innovations and the latest Artificial Intelligence (AI) advances about the emerging nature of AI-based autonomous self-driving driverless cars. Via recent advances in Artificial Intelligence (AI) and Machine Learning (ML), we are nearing the day when vehicles can control themselves and will not require and nor rely upon human intervention to perform their driving tasks (or, that <u>allow</u> for human intervention, but only *require* human intervention in very limited ways).

Similar to my other related books, which I describe in a moment and list the chapters in the Appendix A of this book, I am particularly focused on those advances that pertain to self-driving cars. The phrase "autonomous vehicles" is often used to refer to any kind of vehicle, whether it is ground-based or in the air or sea, and whether it is a cargo hauling trailer truck or a conventional passenger car. Though the aspects described in this book are certainly applicable to all kinds of autonomous vehicles, I am focused more so here on cars.

Indeed, I am especially known for my role in aiding the advancement of self-driving cars, serving currently as the Executive Director of the Cybernetic Self-Driving Cars Institute.. In addition to writing software, designing and developing systems and software for self-driving cars, I also speak and write quite a bit about the topic. This book is a collection of some of my more advanced essays. For those of you that might have seen my essays posted elsewhere, I have updated them and integrated them into this book as one handy cohesive package.

You might be interested in companion books that I have written that provide additional key innovations and fundamentals about self-driving cars. Those books are entitled **"Introduction to Driverless Self-Driving Cars," "Advances in AI and Autonomous Vehicles: Cybernetic Self-Driving Cars," "Self-Driving Cars: "The Mother of All AI Projects," "Innovation and Thought Leadership on Self-Driving Driverless Cars," "New Advances in AI Autonomous Driverless Self-Driving Cars,"** and **"Autonomous Vehicle Driverless Self-Driving Cars and**

Artificial Intelligence" (they are all available via Amazon). See Appendix A of this herein book to see a listing of the chapters covered in those three books.

For the introduction here to this book, I am going to borrow my introduction from those companion books, since it does a good job of laying out the landscape of self-driving cars and my overall viewpoints on the topic. The remainder of the book is all new material that does not appear in the companion books.

INTRODUCTION TO SELF-DRIVING CARS

This is a book about self-driving cars. Someday in the future, we'll all have self-driving cars and this book will perhaps seem antiquated, but right now, we are at the forefront of the self-driving car wave. Daily news bombards us with flashes of new announcements by one car maker or another and leaves the impression that within the next few weeks or maybe months that the self-driving car will be here. A casual non-technical reader would assume from these news flashes that in fact we must be on the cusp of a true self-driving car.

Here's a real news flash: We are still quite a distance from having a true self-driving car. It is years to go before we get there.

Why is that? Because a true self-driving car is akin to a moonshot. In the same manner that getting us to the moon was an incredible feat, likewise can it be said for achieving a true self-driving car. Anybody that suggests or even brashly states that the true self-driving car is nearly here should be viewed with great skepticism. Indeed, you'll see that I often tend to use the word "hogwash" or "crock" when I assess much of the decidedly **fake news** about self-driving cars. Those of us on the inside know that what is often reported to the outside is malarkey. Few of the insiders are willing to say so. I have no such hesitation.

Indeed, I've been writing a popular blog post about self-driving cars and hitting hard on those that try to wave their hands and pretend that we are on the imminent verge of true self-driving cars. For many years, I've been known as the AI Insider. Besides writing about AI, I also develop AI software. I do what I describe. It also gives me insights into what others that are doing AI are really doing versus what it is said they are doing.

Many faithful readers had asked me to pull together my insightful short essays and put them into another book, which you are now holding in your hands.

For those of you that have been reading my essays over the years, this collection not only puts them together into one handy package, I also updated the essays and added new material. For those of you that are new to the topic of self-driving cars and AI, I hope you find these essays approachable and informative. I also tend to have a writing style with a bit of a voice, and so you'll see that I am times have a wry sense of humor and also like to poke at conformity.

As a former professor and founder of an AI research lab, I for many years wrote in the formal language of academic writing. I published in referred journals and served as an editor for several AI journals. This writing here is not of the nature, and I have adopted a different and more informal style for these essays. That being said, I also do mention from time-to-time more rigorous material on AI and encourage you all to dig into those deeper and more formal materials if so interested.

I am also an AI practitioner. This means that I write AI software for a living. Currently, I head-up the Cybernetics Self-Driving Car Institute, where we are developing AI software for self-driving cars. I am excited to also report that my son, also a software engineer, heads-up our Cybernetics Self-Driving Car Lab. What I have helped to start, and for which he is an integral part, ultimately he will carry long into the future after I have retired. My daughter, a marketing whiz, also is integral to our efforts as head of our Marketing group. She too will carry forward the legacy now being formulated.

For those of you that are reading this book and have a penchant for writing code, you might consider taking a look at the open source code available for self-driving cars. This is a handy place to start learning how to develop AI for self-driving cars. There are also many new educational courses spring forth.

There is a growing body of those wanting to learn about and develop self-driving cars, and a growing body of colleges, labs, and other avenues by which you can learn about self-driving cars.

This book will provide a foundation of aspects that I think will get you ready for those kinds of more advanced training opportunities. If you've already taken those classes, you'll likely find these essays especially interesting as they offer a perspective that I am betting few other instructors or faculty offered to you. These are challenging essays that ask you to think beyond the conventional about self-driving cars.

THE MOTHER OF ALL AI PROJECTS

In June 2017, Apple CEO Tim Cook came out and finally admitted that Apple has been working on a self-driving car. As you'll see in my essays, Apple was enmeshed in secrecy about their self-driving car efforts. We have only been able to read the tea leaves and guess at what Apple has been up to. The notion of an iCar has been floating for quite a while, and self-driving engineers and researchers have been signing tight-lipped Non-Disclosure Agreements (NDA's) to work on projects at Apple that were as shrouded in mystery as any military invasion plans might be.

Tim Cook said something that many others in the Artificial Intelligence (AI) field have been saying, namely, the creation of a self-driving car has got to be the mother of all AI projects. In other words, it is in fact a tremendous moonshot for AI. If a self-driving car can be crafted and the AI works as we hope, it means that we have made incredible strides with AI and that therefore it opens many other worlds of potential breakthrough accomplishments that AI can solve.

Is this hyperbole? Am I just trying to make AI seem like a miracle worker and so provide self-aggrandizing statements for those of us writing the AI software for self-driving cars? No, it is not hyperbole. Developing a true self-driving car is really, really, really hard to do. Let me take a moment to explain why. As a side note, I realize that the Apple CEO is known for at times uttering hyperbole, and he had previously said for example that the year 2012 was "the mother of all years," and he had said that the release of iOS 10 was "the mother of all releases" – all of which does suggest he likes to use the handy "mother of" expression. But, I assure you, in terms of true self-driving cars, he has hit the nail on the head. For sure.

When you think about a moonshot and how we got to the moon, there are some identifiable characteristics and those same aspects can be applied to creating a true self-driving car. You'll notice that I keep putting the word "true" in front of the self-driving car expression. I do so because as per my essay about the various levels of self-driving cars (see Chapter 3), there are some self-driving cars that are only somewhat of a self-driving car. The somewhat versions are ones that require a human driver to be ready to intervene. In my view, that's not a true self-driving car. A true self-driving car is one that requires no human driver intervention at all. It is a car that can entirely undertake via automation the driving task without any human driver needed. This is the essence of what is known as a Level 5 self-driving car. We are currently at the Level 2 and Level 3 mark, and not yet at Level 5.

Getting to the moon involved aspects such as having big stretch goals, incremental progress, experimentation, innovation, and so on. Let's review how this applied to the moonshot of the bygone era, and how it applies to the self-driving car moonshot of today.

Big Stretch Goal

Trying to take a human and deliver the human to the moon, and bring them back, safely, was an extremely large stretch goal at the time. No one knew whether it could be done. The technology wasn't available yet. The cost was huge. The determination would need to be fierce. Etc. To reach a Level

5 self-driving car is going to be the same. It is a big stretch goal. We can readily get to the Level 3, and we are able to see the Level 4 just up ahead, but a Level 5 is still an unknown as to if it is doable. It should eventually be doable and in the same way that we thought we'd eventually get to the moon, but when it will occur is a different story.

Incremental Progress

Getting to the moon did not happen overnight in one fell swoop. It took years and years of incremental progress to get there. Likewise for self-driving cars. Google has famously been striving to get to the Level 5, and pretty much been willing to forgo dealing with the intervening levels, but most of the other self-driving car makers are doing the incremental route. Let's get a good Level 2 and a somewhat Level 3 going. Then, let's improve the Level 3 and get a somewhat Level 4 going. Then, let's improve the Level 4 and finally arrive at a Level 5. This seems to be the prevalent way that we are going to achieve the true self-driving car.

Experimentation

You likely know that there were various experiments involved in perfecting the approach and technology to get to the moon. As per making incremental progress, we first tried to see if we could get a rocket to go into space and safety return, then put a monkey in there, then with a human, then we went all the way to the moon but didn't land, and finally we arrived at the mission that actually landed on the moon. Self-driving cars are the same way. We are doing simulations of self-driving cars. We do testing of self-driving cars on private land under controlled situations. We do testing of self-driving cars on public roadways, often having to meet regulatory requirements including for example having an engineer or equivalent in the car to take over the controls if needed. And so on. Experiments big and small are needed to figure out what works and what doesn't.

Innovation

There are already some advances in AI that are allowing us to progress toward self-driving cars. We are going to need even more advances. Innovation in all aspects of technology are going to be required to achieve a true self-driving car. By no means do we already have everything in-hand that we need to get there. Expect new inventions and new approaches, new algorithms, etc.

Setbacks

Most of the pundits are avoiding talking about potential setbacks in the progress toward self-driving cars. Getting to the moon involved many setbacks, some of which you never have heard of and were buried at the time so as to not dampen enthusiasm and funding for getting to the moon. A recurring theme in many of my included essays is that there are going to be setbacks as we try to arrive at a true self-driving car. Take a deep breath and be ready. I just hope the setbacks don't completely stop progress. I am sure that it will cause progress to alter in a manner that we've not yet seen in the self-driving car field. I liken the self-driving car of today to the excitement everyone had for Uber when it first got going. Today, we have a different view of Uber and with each passing day there are more regulations to the ride sharing business and more concerns raised. The darling child only stays a darling until finally that child acts up. It will happen the same with self-driving cars.

SELF-DRIVING CARS CHALLENGES

But what exactly makes things so hard to have a true self-driving car, you might be asking. You have seen cruise control for years and years. You've lately seen cars that can do parallel parking. You've seen YouTube videos of Tesla drivers that put their hands out the window as their car zooms along the highway, and seen to therefore be in a self-driving car. Aren't we just needing to put a few more sensors onto a car and then we'll have in-hand a true self-driving car? Nope.

Consider for a moment the nature of the driving task. We don't just let anyone at any age drive a car. Worldwide, most countries won't license a driver until the age of 18, though many do allow a learner's permit at the age of 15 or 16. Some suggest that a younger age would be physically too small to reach the controls of the car. Though this might be the case, we could easily adjust the controls to allow for younger aged and thus smaller stature. It's not their physical size that matters. It's their cognitive development that matters.

To drive a car, you need to be able to reason about the car, what the car can and cannot do. You need to know how to operate the car. You need to know about how other cars on the road drive. You need to know what is allowed in driving such as speed limits and driving within marked lanes. You need to be able to react to situations and be able to avoid getting into accidents. You need to ascertain when to hit your brakes, when to steer clear of a pedestrian, and how to keep from ramming that motorcyclist that just cut you off.

Many of us had taken courses on driving. We studied about driving and took driver training. We had to take a test and pass it to be able to drive. The point being that though most adults take the driving task for granted, and we often "mindlessly" drive our cars, there is a significant amount of cognitive effort that goes into driving a car. After a while, it becomes second nature. You don't especially think about how you drive, you just do it. But, if you watch a novice driver, say a teenager learning to drive, you suddenly realize that there is a lot more complexity to it than we seem to realize.

Furthermore, driving is a very serious task. I recall when my daughter and son first learned to drive. They are both very conscientious people. They wanted to make sure that whatever they did, they did well, and that they did not harm anyone. Every day, when you get into a car, it is probably around 4,000 pounds of hefty metal and plastics (about two tons), and it is a lethal weapon. Think about it. You drive down the street in an object that weighs two tons and with the engine it can accelerate and ram into anything you want to hit. The damage a car can inflict is very scary. Both my children were surprised that they were being given the right to maneuver this monster of a beast that could cause tremendous harm entirely by merely letting go of the steering wheel for a moment or taking your eyes off the road.

In fact, in the United States alone there are about 30,000 deaths per year by auto accidents, which is around 100 per day. Given that there are about 263 million cars in the United States, I am actually more amazed that the number of fatalities is not a lot higher. During my morning commute, I look at all the thousands of cars on the freeway around me, and I think that if all of them decided to go zombie and drive in a crazy maniac way, there would be many people dead. Somehow, incredibly, each day, most people drive relatively safely. To me, that's a miracle right there. Getting millions and millions of people to be safe and sane when behind the wheel of a two ton mobile object, it's a feat that we as a society should admire with pride.

So, hopefully you are in agreement that the driving task requires a great deal of cognition. You don't' need to be especially smart to drive a car, and we've done quite a bit to make car driving viable for even the average dolt. There isn't an IQ test that you need to take to drive a car. If you can read and write, and pass a test, you pretty much can legally drive a car. There are of course some that drive a car and are not legally permitted to do so, plus there are private areas such as farms where drivers are young, but for public roadways in the United States, you can be generally of average intelligence (or less) and be able to legally drive.

This though makes it seem like the cognitive effort must not be much. If the cognitive effort was truly hard, wouldn't we only have Einstein's that could drive a car? We have made sure to keep the driving task as simple as we can, by making the controls easy and relatively standardized, and by having roads that are relatively standardized, and so on. It is as though Disneyland has put their Autopia into the real-world, by us all as a society agreeing that roads will be a certain way, and we'll all abide by the various rules of driving.

A modest cognitive task by a human is still something that stymies AI. You certainly know that AI has been able to beat chess players and be good at other kinds of games. This type of narrow cognition is not what car driving is about. Car driving is much wider. It requires knowledge about the world, which a chess playing AI system does not need to know. The cognitive aspects of driving are on the one hand seemingly simple, but at the same time require layer upon layer of knowledge about cars, people, roads, rules, and a myriad of other "common sense" aspects. We don't have any AI systems today that have that same kind of breadth and depth of awareness and knowledge.

As revealed in my essays, the self-driving car of today is using trickery to do particular tasks. It is all very narrow in operation. Plus, it currently assumes that a human driver is ready to intervene. It is like a child that we have taught to stack blocks, but we are needed to be right there in case the child stacks them too high and they begin to fall over. AI of today is brittle, it is narrow, and it does not approach the cognitive abilities of humans. This is why the true self-driving car is somewhere out in the future.

Another aspect to the driving task is that it is not solely a mind exercise. You do need to use your senses to drive. You use your eyes a vision sensors to see the road ahead. You vision capability is like a streaming video, which your brain needs to continually analyze as you drive. Where is the road? Is there a pedestrian in the way? Is there another car ahead of you? Your senses are relying a flood of info to your brain. Self-driving cars are trying to do the same, by using cameras, radar, ultrasound, and lasers. This is an attempt at mimicking how humans have senses and sensory apparatus.

Thus, the driving task is mental and physical. You use your senses, you use your arms and legs to manipulate the controls of the car, and you use your brain to assess the sensory info and direct your limbs to act upon the controls of the car. This all happens instantly. If you've ever perhaps gotten something in your eye and only had one eye available to drive with, you suddenly realize how dependent upon vision you are. If you have a broken foot with a cast, you suddenly realize how hard it is to control the brake pedal and the accelerator. If you've taken medication and your brain is maybe sluggish, you suddenly realize how much mental strain is required to drive a car.

An AI system that plays chess only needs to be focused on playing chess. The physical aspects aren't important because usually a human moves the chess pieces or the chessboard is shown on an electronic display. Using AI for a more life-and-death task such as analyzing MRI images of patients, this again does not require physical capabilities and instead is done by examining images of bits.

Driving a car is a true life-and-death task. It is a use of AI that can easily and at any moment produce death. For those colleagues of mine that are developing this AI, as am I, we need to keep in mind the somber aspects of this. We are producing software that will have in its virtual hands the lives of the occupants of the car, and the lives of those in other nearby cars, and the lives of nearby pedestrians, etc. Chess is not usually a life-or-death matter.

Driving is all around us. Cars are everywhere. Most of today's AI applications involve only a small number of people. Or, they are behind the scenes and we as humans have other recourse if the AI messes up. AI that is driving a car at 80 miles per hour on a highway had better not mess up. The consequences are grave. Multiply this by the number of cars, if we could put magically self-driving into every car in the USA, we'd have AI running in the 263 million cars. That's a lot of AI spread around. This is AI on a massive scale that we are not doing today and that offers both promise and potential peril.

There are some that want AI for self-driving cars because they envision a world without any car accidents. They envision a world in which there is no car congestion and all cars cooperate with each other. These are wonderful utopian visions.

They are also very misleading. The adoption of self-driving cars is going to be incremental and not overnight. We cannot economically just junk all existing cars. Nor are we going to be able to affordably retrofit existing cars. It is more likely that self-driving cars will be built into new cars and that over many years of gradual replacement of existing cars that we'll see the mix of self-driving cars become substantial in the real-world.

In these essays, I have tried to offer technological insights without being overly technical in my description, and also blended the business, societal, and economic aspects too. Technologists need to consider the non-technological impacts of what they do. Non-technologists should be aware of what is being developed.

We all need to work together to collectively be prepared for the enormous disruption and transformative aspects of true self-driving cars. We all need to be involved in this mother of all AI projects.

WHAT THIS BOOK PROVIDES

What does this book provide to you? It introduces many of the key elements about self-driving cars and does so with an AI based perspective. I weave together technical and non-technical aspects, readily going from being concerned about the cognitive capabilities of the driving task and how the technology is embodying this into self-driving cars, and in the next breath I discuss the societal and economic aspects.

They are all intertwined because that's the way reality is. You cannot separate out the technology per se, and instead must consider it within the milieu of what is being invented and innovated, and do so with a mindset towards the contemporary mores and culture that shape what we are doing and what we hope to do.

WHY THIS BOOK

I wrote this book to try and bring to the public view many aspects about self-driving cars that nobody seems to be discussing.

For business leaders that are either involved in making self-driving cars or that are going to leverage self-driving cars, I hope that this book will enlighten you as to the risks involved and ways in which you should be strategizing about how to deal with those risks.

For entrepreneurs, startups and other businesses that want to enter into the self-driving car market that is emerging, I hope this book sparks your interest in doing so, and provides some sense of what might be prudent to pursue.

For researchers that study self-driving cars, I hope this book spurs your interest in the risks and safety issues of self-driving cars, and also nudges you toward conducting research on those aspects.

For students in computer science or related disciplines, I hope this book will provide you with interesting and new ideas and material, for which you might conduct research or provide some career direction insights for you.

For AI companies and high-tech companies pursuing self-driving cars, this book will hopefully broaden your view beyond just the mere coding and development needed to make self-driving cars.

For all readers, I hope that you will find the material in this book to be stimulating. Some of it will be repetitive of things you already know. But I am pretty sure that you'll also find various eureka moments whereby you'll discover a new technique or approach that you had not earlier thought of. I am also betting that there will be material that forces you to rethink some of your current practices.

I am not saying you will suddenly have an epiphany and change what you are doing. I do think though that you will reconsider or perhaps revisit what you are doing.

For anyone choosing to use this book for teaching purposes, please take a look at my suggestions for doing so, as described in the Appendix. I have found the material handy in courses that I have taught, and likewise other faculty have told me that they have found the material handy, in some cases as extended readings and in other instances as a core part of their course (depending on the nature of the class).

In my writing for this book, I have tried carefully to blend both the practitioner and the academic styles of writing. It is not as dense as is typical academic journal writing, but at the same time offers depth by going into the nuances and trade-offs of various practices.

The word "deep" is in vogue today, meaning getting deeply into a subject or topic, and so is the word "unpack" which means to tease out the underlying aspects of a subject or topic. I have sought to offer material that addresses an issue or topic by going relatively deeply into it and make sure that it is well unpacked.

Finally, in any book about AI, it is difficult to use our everyday words without having some of them be misinterpreted. Specifically, it is easy to anthropomorphize AI. When I say that an AI system "knows" something, I do not want you to construe that the AI system has sentience and "knows" in the same way that humans do. They aren't that way, as yet. I have tried to use quotes around such words from time-to-time to emphasize that the words I am using should not be misinterpreted to ascribe true human intelligence to the AI systems that we know of today. If I used quotes around all such words, the book would be very difficult to read, and so I am doing so judiciously. Please keep that in mind as you read the material, thanks.

Lance B. Eliot

COMPANION BOOKS

If you find this material of interest, you might want to also see my other books on self-driving cars, entitled:

1. **"Introduction to Driverless Self-Driving Cars"** by Dr. Lance Eliot

2. **"Innovation and Thought Leadership on Self-Driving Driverless Cars"** by Dr. Lance Eliot

3. **"Advances in AI and Autonomous Vehicles: Cybernetic Self-Driving Cars"** by Dr. Lance Eliot

4. ***"Self-Driving Cars: The Mother of All AI Projects"*** by Dr. Lance Eliot

5. **"New Advances in AI Autonomous Driverless Self-Driving Cars"** by Dr. Lance Eliot

6. **"Autonomous Vehicle Driverless Self-Driving Cars and Artificial Intelligence"** by Dr. Lance Eliot and Michael B. Eliot

All of the above books are available on Amazon and at other major global booksellers.

Lance B. Eliot

CHAPTER 1

ELIOT FRAMEWORK FOR AI SELF-DRIVING CARS

Lance B. Eliot

CHAPTER 1

ELIOT FRAMEWORK FOR AI SELF-DRIVING CARS

This chapter is a core foundational aspect for understanding AI self-driving cars and I have used this same chapter in several of my other books to introduce the reader to essential elements of this field. Once you've read this chapter, you'll be prepared to read the rest of the material since the foundational essence of the components of autonomous AI driverless self-driving cars will have been established for you.

―――――――

When I give presentations about self-driving cars and teach classes on the topic, I have found it helpful to provide a framework around which the various key elements of self-driving cars can be understood and organized (see diagram at the end of this chapter). The framework needs to be simple enough to convey the overarching elements, but at the same time not so simple that it belies the true complexity of self-driving cars. As such, I am going to describe the framework here and try to offer in a thousand words (or more!) what the framework diagram itself intends to portray.

The core elements on the diagram are numbered for ease of reference. The numbering does not suggest any kind of prioritization of the elements. Each element is crucial. Each element has a purpose, and otherwise would not be included in the framework. For some self-driving cars, a particular element might be more important or somehow distinguished in comparison to other self-driving cars.

You could even use the framework to rate a particular self-driving car, doing so by gauging how well it performs in each of the elements of the framework. I will describe each of the elements, one at a time. After doing so, I'll discuss aspects that illustrate how the elements interact and perform during the overall effort of a self-driving car.

At the Cybernetic Self-Driving Car Institute, we use the framework to keep track of what we are working on, and how we are developing software that fills in what is needed to achieve Level 5 self-driving cars.

D-01: Sensor Capture

Let's start with the one element that often gets the most attention in the press about self-driving cars, namely, the sensory devices for a self-driving car.

On the framework, the box labeled as D-01 indicates "Sensor Capture" and refers to the processes of the self-driving car that involve collecting data from the myriad of sensors that are used for a self-driving car. The types of devices typically involved are listed, such as the use of mono cameras, stereo cameras, LIDAR devices, radar systems, ultrasonic devices, GPS, IMU, and so on.

These devices are tasked with obtaining data about the status of the self-driving car and the world around it. Some of the devices are continually providing updates, while others of the devices await an indication by the self-driving car that the device is supposed to collect data. The data might be first transformed in some fashion by the device itself, or it might instead be fed directly into the sensor capture as raw data. At that point, it might be up to the sensor capture processes to do transformations on the data. This all varies depending upon the nature of the devices being used and how the devices were designed and developed.

D-02: Sensor Fusion

Imagine that your eyeballs receive visual images, your nose receives odors, your ears receive sounds, and in essence each of your distinct sensory devices is getting some form of input. The input befits the nature of the device. Likewise, for a self-driving car, the cameras provide visual images, the radar returns radar reflections, and so on.

Each device provides the data as befits what the device does.

At some point, using the analogy to humans, you need to merge together what your eyes see, what your nose smells, what your ears hear, and piece it all together into a larger sense of what the world is all about and what is happening around you. Sensor fusion is the action of taking the singular aspects from each of the devices and putting them together into a larger puzzle.

Sensor fusion is a tough task. There are some devices that might not be working at the time of the sensor capture. Or, there might some devices that are unable to report well what they have detected. Again, using a human analogy, suppose you are in a dark room and so your eyes cannot see much. At that point, you might need to rely more so on your ears and what you hear. The same is true for a self-driving car. If the cameras are obscured due to snow and sleet, it might be that the radar can provide a greater indication of what the external conditions consist of.

In the case of a self-driving car, there can be a plethora of such sensory devices. Each is reporting what it can. Each might have its difficulties. Each might have its limitations, such as how far ahead it can detect an object. All of these limitations need to be considered during the sensor fusion task.

D-03: Virtual World Model

For humans, we presumably keep in our minds a model of the world around us when we are driving a car. In your mind, you know that the car is going at say 60 miles per hour and that you are on a freeway. You have a model in your mind that your car is surrounded by other cars, and that there are lanes to the freeway. Your model is not only based on what you can see, hear, etc., but also what you know about the nature of the world. You know that at any moment that car ahead of you can smash on its brakes, or the car behind you can ram into your car, or that the truck in the next lane might swerve into your lane.

The AI of the self-driving car needs to have a virtual world model, which it then keeps updated with whatever it is receiving from the sensor fusion, which received its input from the sensor capture and the sensory devices.

D-04: System Action Plan

By having a virtual world model, the AI of the self-driving car is able to keep track of where the car is and what is happening around the car. In addition, the AI needs to determine what to do next. Should the self-driving car hit its brakes? Should the self-driving car stay in its lane or swerve into the lane to the left? Should the self-driving car accelerate or slow down?

A system action plan needs to be prepared by the AI of the self-driving car. The action plan specifies what actions should be taken. The actions need to pertain to the status of the virtual world model. Plus, the actions need to be realizable.

This realizability means that the AI cannot just assert that the self-driving car should suddenly sprout wings and fly. Instead, the AI must be bound by whatever the self-driving car can actually do, such as coming to a halt in a distance of X feet at a speed of Y miles per hour, rather than perhaps asserting that the self-driving car come to a halt in 0 feet as though it could instantaneously come to a stop while it is in motion.

D-05: Controls Activation

The system action plan is implemented by activating the controls of the car to act according to what the plan stipulates. This might mean that the accelerator control is commanded to increase the speed of the car. Or, the steering control is commanded to turn the steering wheel 30 degrees to the left or right.

One question arises as to whether or not the controls respond as they are commanded to do. In other words, suppose the AI has commanded the accelerator to increase, but for some reason it does not do so. Or, maybe it tries to do so, but the speed of the car does not increase. The controls activation feeds back into the virtual world model, and simultaneously the virtual world model is getting updated from the sensors, the sensor capture, and the sensor fusion. This allows the AI to ascertain what has taken place as a result of the controls being commanded to take some kind of action.

By the way, please keep in mind that though the diagram seems to have a linear progression to it, the reality is that these are all aspects of the self-driving car that are happening in parallel and simultaneously. The sensors are capturing data, meanwhile the sensor fusion is taking place, meanwhile the virtual model is being updated, meanwhile the system action plan is being formulated and reformulated, meanwhile the controls are being activated.

This is the same as a human being that is driving a car. They are eyeballing the road, meanwhile they are fusing in their mind the sights, sounds, etc., meanwhile their mind is updating their model of the world around them, meanwhile they are formulating an action plan of what to do, and meanwhile they are pushing their foot onto the pedals and steering the car. In the normal course of driving a car, you are doing all of these at once. I mention this so that when you look at the diagram, you will think of the boxes as processes that are all happening at the same time, and not as though only one happens and then the next.

They are shown diagrammatically in a simplistic manner to help comprehend what is taking place. You though should also realize that they are working in parallel and simultaneous with each other. This is a tough aspect in that the inter-element communications involve latency and other aspects that must be taken into account. There can be delays in one element updating and then sharing its latest status with other elements.

D-06: Automobile & CAN

Contemporary cars use various automotive electronics and a Controller Area Network (CAN) to serve as the components that underlie the driving aspects of a car. There are Electronic Control Units (ECU's) which control subsystems of the car, such as the engine, the brakes, the doors, the windows, and so on.

The elements D-01, D-02, D-03, D-04, D-05 are layered on top of the D-06, and must be aware of the nature of what the D-06 is able to do and not do.

D-07: In-Car Commands

Humans are going to be occupants in self-driving cars. In a Level 5 self-driving car, there must be some form of communication that takes place between the humans and the self-driving car. For example, I go into a self-driving car and tell it that I want to be driven over to Disneyland, and along the way I want to stop at In-and-Out Burger. The self-driving car now parses what I've said and tries to then establish a means to carry out my wishes.

In-car commands can happen at any time during a driving journey. Though my example was about an in-car command when I first got into my self-driving car, it could be that while the self-driving car is carrying out the journey that I change my mind. Perhaps after getting stuck in traffic, I tell the self-driving car to forget about getting the burgers and just head straight over to the theme park. The self-driving car needs to be alert to in-car commands throughout the journey.

D-08: VX2 Communications

We will ultimately have self-driving cars communicating with each other, doing so via V2V (Vehicle-to-Vehicle) communications. We will also have self-driving cars that communicate with the roadways and other aspects of the transportation infrastructure, doing so via V2I (Vehicle-to-Infrastructure).

The variety of ways in which a self-driving car will be communicating with other cars and infrastructure is being called V2X, whereby the letter X means whatever else we identify as something that a car should or would want to communicate with. The V2X communications will be taking place simultaneous with everything else on the diagram, and those other elements will need to incorporate whatever it gleans from those V2X communications.

D-09: Deep Learning

The use of Deep Learning permeates all other aspects of the self-driving car. The AI of the self-driving car will be using deep learning to do a better job at the systems action plan, and at the controls activation, and at the sensor fusion, and so on.

Currently, the use of artificial neural networks is the most prevalent form of deep learning. Based on large swaths of data, the neural networks attempt to "learn" from the data and therefore direct the efforts of the self-driving car accordingly.

D-10: Tactical AI

Tactical AI is the element of dealing with the moment-to-moment driving of the self-driving car. Is the self-driving car staying in its lane of the freeway? Is the car responding appropriately to the controls commands? Are the sensory devices working?

For human drivers, the tactical equivalent can be seen when you watch a novice driver such as a teenager that is first driving. They are focused on the mechanics of the driving task, keeping their eye on the road while also trying to properly control the car.

D-11: Strategic AI

The Strategic AI aspects of a self-driving car are dealing with the larger picture of what the self-driving car is trying to do. If I had asked that the self-driving car take me to Disneyland, there is an overall journey map that needs to be kept and maintained.

There is an interaction between the Strategic AI and the Tactical AI. The Strategic AI is wanting to keep on the mission of the driving, while the Tactical AI is focused on the particulars underway in the driving effort. If the Tactical AI seems to wander away from the overarching mission, the Strategic AI wants to see why and get things back on track. If the Tactical AI realizes that there is something amiss on the self-driving car, it needs to alert the Strategic AI accordingly and have an adjustment to the overarching mission that is underway.

D-12: Self-Aware AI

Very few of the self-driving cars being developed are including a Self-Aware AI element, which we at the Cybernetic Self-Driving Car Institute believe is crucial to Level 5 self-driving cars.

The Self-Aware AI element is intended to watch over itself, in the sense that the AI is making sure that the AI is working as intended. Suppose you had a human driving a car, and they were starting to drive erratically. Hopefully, their own self-awareness would make them realize they themselves are driving poorly, such as perhaps starting to fall asleep after having been driving for hours on end. If you had a passenger in the car, they might be able to alert the driver if the driver is starting to do something amiss. This is exactly what the Self-Aware

AI element tries to do, it becomes the overseer of the AI, and tries to detect when the AI has become faulty or confused, and then find ways to overcome the issue.

D-13: Economic

The economic aspects of a self-driving car are not per se a technology aspect of a self-driving car, but the economics do indeed impact the nature of a self-driving car. For example, the cost of outfitting a self-driving car with every kind of possible sensory device is prohibitive, and so choices need to be made about which devices are used. And, for those sensory devices chosen, whether they would have a full set of features or a more limited set of features.

We are going to have self-driving cars that are at the low-end of a consumer cost point, and others at the high-end of a consumer cost point. You cannot expect that the self-driving car at the low-end is going to be as robust as the one at the high-end. I realize that many of the self-driving car pundits are acting as though all self-driving cars will be the same, but they won't be. Just like anything else, we are going to have self-driving cars that have a range of capabilities. Some will be better than others. Some will be safer than others. This is the way of the real-world, and so we need to be thinking about the economics aspects when considering the nature of self-driving cars.

D-14: Societal

This component encompasses the societal aspects of AI which also impacts the technology of self-driving cars. For example, the famous Trolley Problem involves what choices should a self-driving car make when faced with life-and-death matters. If the self-driving car is about to either hit a child standing in the roadway, or instead ram into a tree at the side of the road and possibly kill the humans in the self-driving car, which choice should be made?

We need to keep in mind the societal aspects will underlie the AI of the self-driving car. Whether we are aware of it explicitly or not, the AI will have embedded into it various societal assumptions.

D-15: Innovation

I included the notion of innovation into the framework because we can anticipate that whatever a self-driving car consists of, it will continue to be innovated over time. The self-driving cars coming out in the next several years will undoubtedly be different and less innovative than the versions that come out in ten years hence, and so on.

Framework Overall

For those of you that want to learn about self-driving cars, you can potentially pick a particular element and become specialized in that aspect. Some engineers are focusing on the sensory devices. Some engineers focus on the controls activation. And so on. There are specialties in each of the elements.

Researchers are likewise specializing in various aspects. For example, there are researchers that are using Deep Learning to see how best it can be used for sensor fusion. There are other researchers that are using Deep Learning to derive good System Action Plans. Some are studying how to develop AI for the Strategic aspects of the driving task, while others are focused on the Tactical aspects.

A well-prepared all-around software developer that is involved in self-driving cars should be familiar with all of the elements, at least to the degree that they know what each element does. This is important since whatever piece of the pie that the software developer works on, they need to be knowledgeable about what the other elements are doing.

Lance B. Eliot

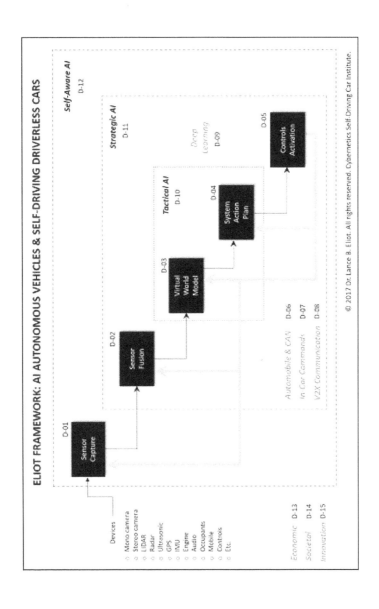

Lance B. Eliot

CHAPTER 2

KINETOSIS ANTI-MOTION SICKNESS FOR SELF-DRIVING CARS

Lance B. Eliot

CHAPTER 2

KINETOSIS ANTI-MOTION SICKNESS FOR SELF-DRIVING CARS

When my children were in their teens, I used to shuttle them all around town for various before-school and after-school activities. My son would need to get over to the baseball field for practices and games. My daughter was in a performing arts program as a lead actress and would need to get to her rehearsals and performances. Most parents nowadays comment about how busy their children are, and that there is not a moment to spare in their schedules. This was certainly true in the case of my kids.

To try and make use of every moment of time, my son and daughter would try to get homework done while in the car. Thus, rather than just looking out the car window to enjoy the surroundings, or rather than idly chatting or maybe calling a friend on their cell phones, they figured that the "quiet" time in the car would be perfect for trying to get some of those math homework problems done or perhaps do some studying for their history or science classes. By doing so, they were aiming to keep from having to stay up until midnight to get their homework done after finishing up all the extracurricular efforts of the afternoon and early evening.

In theory, it should have been very doable for them to work on their homework in the car.

Unfortunately, it was not always the case. From time to time, one of them or both would succumb to motion sickness. I'm sure you've had it happen to you too. For some people, the motion of the car causes them to feel queasy, especially when trying to read or write while the car is moving along. The symptoms and reactions differ by person, and differ by the circumstance. You might feel dizzy. Your stomach might churn. Perhaps vertigo sets in. The worst is a tinge of nausea that then becomes an actual vomit laden outcome. Yuk!

This motion sickness is also known as kinetosis.

More commonly, some refer to it as car sickness, or travel sickness, and it is similar to seasickness except you are in a car rather than a ship at sea. Remember when people used to frequently get motion sickness while flying in a plane? Today, we still have those airsickness bags at each seat of the plane. Of course, there isn't much of airsickness happening these days. The earlier era of flying for the general public often had planes that were unable to assure a smooth ride, and the air on the planes was not well controlled, all of which led to a lot of airsickness flyers. That's pretty much a thing of the past now.

Motion sickness in a car is not much discussed today either. That's because most cars aren't amenable to doing the kind of reading and writing that I mentioned that my children tried to do. The seats in a car are all facing forward, the space is cramped, and so any kind of serious studying is not really encouraged per se. If we somehow tomorrow made a governmental declaration that you must study while in your car, imagine how much the volume of motion sickness among the population would rise. We'd have an epidemic of car motion sickness!

Well, maybe we are headed in that same direction. Not due to a government mandate, but instead due to the new opportunities for being able to study, or read, or sleep, or whatever while in a car. This can all be made possible due to the advent of self-driving cars. If a car does not need a human driver, the prediction is that passengers in cars will begin to use cars for purposes such as reading, writing, sleeping, etc. If that happens, it means that a lot of people that today are not particularly placing themselves into a motion sickness situation, will now be directly immersed in a motion sickness likely circumstance.

Suppose you currently drive to work and it's an hour long commute. Without the need to be the driver, since the self-driving car's AI is doing the driving for you, what will you do in that car for an hour long commute? Watch a movie? Talk on the phone? Read a book? Catch a nap? I'm betting that any of those actions will increase your odds of experiencing motion sickness.

Why would you tend toward motion sickness? There is a lot of debate about what actually causes car-related motion sickness. Drivers of cars don't seem to get motion sickness, while passengers do. Passengers in the back seat tend to get it more than a passenger that sits next to the driver. Some say that adults get it more than children, while others say that children get it more than adults. Generally, most experts would agree that the mainstay of the issue is that there is a mismatch between what the human is visually perceiving and what their internal bodily organs are telling them. The vestibular system and its sense of movement is often at odds with what the visual system is saying.

Let's unpack that aspect. A driver is looking intently (we hope!) at the roadway and is visually well aware that the car is moving forward. Their internal vestibular system is saying that same thing. Thus, the alignment is good. A passenger in the car that is reading a book would have their visual focus on the book, and therefore not be looking out the window, and would be unlike the car driver. The eyes and visual system of the reading passenger are now at odds with what the internal vestibular system is saying. The internal system is saying that there is rapid forward motion, but the eyes are looking at something that appears to be unmoving. It is believed by many experts that this mismatch is what contributes mightily toward motion sickness while in the car.

A passenger seated next to the driver is able to look up and around, and visually realign with what the internal vestibular system is feeling. But a passenger in the back seat has a harder time doing the same thing. Their view of the world is usually blocked by the front seats and other aspects of the interior of the car. They cannot readily convince their visual system that the car is in motion. It is believed that this is why those in the back seats are more prone to motion sickness than the passenger in the front seat.

Now, I am sure that some of you are saying that you never get motion sickness in a car. You are probably saying it is hogwash that reading might lead to getting car sickness, because you read full novels all the time while being a passenger in a car. This leads us to another element of car motion sickness. Namely, DNA. Some experts assert that the proneness to car motion sickness might be hereditary. Maybe your genes are such that you don't get car motion sickness. Meanwhile, maybe other people with different DNA are more prone to it. Some might have DNA that seems to prevent it, some might have DNA that tends towards average chances of car motion sickness, and some might have genes that are very susceptible to car motion sickness. This is one explanation for the variability as to whom gets within its grip.

So far, we have the factor of DNA, and we have the factor of the misalignment between your visual system and your vestibular system. Another factor that I've not yet explicitly called out, which was hidden somewhat, involves the design of the car itself. Recall that I mentioned that back seat passengers could not readily look around to visually get caught up with the motion of the car. If we could somehow redesign the car so that those back passengers had a more ready visual way to see the car motion, maybe they would be less prone to getting car motion sickness.

There are more factors too! Sometimes while in a car, you've probably seem someone that was starting to get motion sickness and they rolled down a window to get fresh air. After doing so, they might then say that they avoided going deeply into the motion sickness by having taken gulps of nice clean air. If they were also looking out the window, we might not be sure if it was truly the air or whether it was because they changed their visual attention.

I am sure that you though have seen people that adjust the air conditioning in the car and then say that they avoided car motion sickness. In that case, they did not look out the window, and so we might reasonably conclude that the air in the car was a key factor related to their car motion sickness. Let's go ahead and then say that air and the flow of air might be considered an additional factor for the motion sickness issue.

Another factor can be the nature of the motion of the car. When a car is zooming along on an open highway, you tend not to see people getting as car sick. If the car is stuck in stop-and-go traffic, it seems that people tend toward the car motion sickness. On curves, it seems that people tend to get car motion sickness. I remember one time we were driving up to the mountains to go skiing, and the trip up the beautiful mountain in the car was actually a horrible experience because there were lots of switchbacks, steep and sharp curves, and the kids became human vomit comets.

In recap, here are some key factors that seem to relate to car motion sickness:

- Visually being able to see the car motion
- Inner ear or vestibular sense of car motion
- DNA or hereditary aspects
- Interior design of the car
- Air flow within the car
- Motion of the car (smooth versus choppy, straight versus turning)
- Task being undertaken (reading, writing, sleeping, etc.)
- How you are positioned in the car (direction facing, sitting up or laying down, etc.)
- Age
- Other

I snuck onto the list the factor of age, though as I say the jury is still out about whether adults or children are more or less susceptible of each other.

What does all of this have to do with AI self-driving cars?

At the Cybernetic Self-Driving Car Institute, we recognize that car motion sickness could be a highly significant detractor from the adoption of self-driving cars, and we are aiming to do something about this before it becomes a huge problem.

If the public finds that being in a self-driving car leads to massive amounts of car motion sickness, we doubt that the public will be willing to have or use or buy a self-driving car. They won't perceive the worthiness of the self-driving capability when all they do is get sick while in the car.

Now, you might argue that all people would need to do is pretend that they are driving the car. In essence, they would just need to face forward, look out at the road, and not read, write, or sleep. That solves the problem!

Not quite. Though it might be cool to have a self-driving car so that you don't have to drive, if it also means that you need to sit like a statue and cannot "enjoy" the new freedoms of not having to drive, it will really dampen the acceptance of self-driving cars.

I realize some of you are thinking, well, just take a drug. We often see people taking Dramamine or similar anti-motion sickness medications while on a ship or a plane. Suppose we just tell people that travel in self-driving cars that they need to have a large bottle of pills to medicate themselves if they feel car motion sickness coming on.

Though I am sure that the drug companies would like this, I am not so sure we want people to regularly be taking those kinds of medications. Imagine if every day during your commute in the morning you medicated, and again when you went home at night. And, you had your kids taking the pills too. We don't really know what kinds of adverse consequences we might see. The prolonged use and the accumulation of the medications in our systems might produce some bad results.

One aspect that we can more readily adjust would be the interior design of the self-driving car.

Currently, conventional cars have a steering wheel, pedals, dashboard, and so on. Presumably, with a true Level 5 self-driving car, you don't need any of that stuff (there is an ongoing debate about this aspect, as to whether even if the human does not need to drive, whether or not the capability to be able drive via controls should be included or not).

What should we do then with the interior space of the car if for a self-driving car we don't need all of the equipment and space devoted to a human driving the car?

Some concept versions of future self-driving cars have envisioned that the interior consists of four seats, two that are the front seats but are now facing to the back, and two back seats facing forward. This allows four passengers to face each other, presumably to carry on dialogue and enjoy each other's company. Other versions of the interior have four seats that all swivel, and therefore each passenger can aim in whatever direction they wish.

How much will this lessen the chances of car motion sickness, you might wonder. Aha, some say that it will actually increase the chances of motion sickness. If people are facing backwards in a forward driven self-driving car, their sensory conflict will be worsened. If they can swivel at their own preference, they will make themselves dizzy like in a Mad Tea Cup ride at a theme park.

Another aspect of the concept self-driving cars is that they will not have any windows at all. The belief is that people in a self-driving car don't need windows since the AI is doing the driving. By removing the windows, the passengers will have privacy in their self-driving car. This makes sense for example if you are planning on doing a lot of sleeping while in your self-driving car. You wouldn't want windows that let people see you asleep, and if you are in your PJ's then for sure you don't want them watching you!

Aha, once again though this might worsen the car motion sickness potential. No windows, no ability to look outside and get your visual system coordinated with your inner system. No problem, some say, we'll just put display screens inside the self-driving car. We could even line the entire interior with screens. We could then have the self-driving car cameras display onto those screens. Presumably, you would now "see" that you are in motion. This assumes that looking out a window at the real-world is the same kind of visual result as looking at a projected version of the real-world via cameras. I'd say the jury is out on this for now.

Alright, then we'll use frosted glass. Or maybe have windows but build in special shades that can open or close to allow for privacy within the self-driving car. Indeed, some concept self-driving cars have much larger windows than we have even on conventional cars. Maybe passengers in a self-driving car will want maximum amount of windows, some think.

There are some researchers that are using simulated driving environments to try and gauge how people will react to these different kinds of interior designs. They put them into a car simulator and try different aspects. Windows versus no windows. Bursts of air. Twisting seats. Light bars. Screens. Seat vibrations. And so on.

Keep in mind that our current design of cars is oriented to the car driver. In other words, the whole premise is that cars are designed for the human driver. You have to have a human driver. You don't have to have human passengers. With a self-driving car (a true Level 5), you don't have to have a human driver. You can have human passengers, though that's not needed per se. Thus, many say that we are mistaken if we don't redesign the interior of the self-driving. We would be carrying forward a design that no longer is applicable, or at least we could possibly find a more suitable design.

Estimates by researchers are that if we don't redesign car interiors for self-driving cars, we might see around 15-20% of passengers that will be getting car motion sickness. Some say it is less, more like toward 5%, while others say it is higher such as one-third of all passengers. It is hard to say. I think it is safe to say that if we don't do anything, we are definitely going to have more car motion sickness with self-driving cars.

When I make such a statement, I realize you might be asking why does the self-driving car make a difference in this car motion sickness calculation? It is mainly because we now have what were once drivers that now will be passengers, and thus we are increasing the number of passengers in the average car ride, and removing the human driver that otherwise wasn't getting car motion sickness. And, if you assume that the amount of time we spend in cars is going to go up, since with a self-driving car we can sleep in it and use it all the time, we then are further increasing the chances and frequency of potential car motion sickness.

Many are saying that the self-driving car will be our new living rooms. It will be our second living space, while our first living space is our home or apartment. For some people, it could be that they consider their self-driving car as their first living space and they merely "rideshare" a physical place to take a shower or whatever, meanwhile literally living out of their self-driving car.

Does the AI of the self-driving car come to play in this?

So far, if we only look at the interior design, the AI itself is not playing any particular role.

Where the AI does come to play is one of the other crucial factors that was mentioned, the motion of the car.

Currently, much of the AI self-driving car capabilities are driving a car like a novice driver. The self-driving car tends to be doing abrupt starts and stops. The AI is not sophisticated enough yet to be able to figure out a smooth drive.

We are purposely advancing the self-driving AI to be able to try and achieve a smoother ride, doing so not only for overall comfort of the passengers, but as a way too to help mitigate the chances of car motion sickness. In freeway stop-and-go traffic, you can either drive a car in a staggered fashion, or if you are clever you can get the motion more toward a smoother sensation. That's what we believe the AI should be able to do.

A goal then for the AI is to try and avoid low-frequency motion patterns, for example, and other patterns such as fast and sharp turns, and so on.

Should it do this all the time?

The AI could do so all of the time, or it could also gauge when to do so.

The AI can be observing the traffic situation and judge accordingly whether to invoke the anti-motion sickness driving mode. Furthermore, the AI could ask the passengers if they are feeling a bit of motion sickness, and then go into the anti-motion sickness driving mode. And, if you are willing to go the Big Brother kind of route, suppose the AI has a camera facing to the interior and can look at the faces of the passengers and automatically detect the signs of motion sickness coming on, and then without having to ask the passengers that the AI opts to go ahead and switch into the anti-motion sickness mode.

The right answer to the car motion sickness issue would seem to be that we need to get ready for it, we need to acknowledge now that it is an upcoming problem, and we need to consider the design of the self-driving car, along with incorporating anti-motion sickness driving capabilities into the AI of the self-driving car. If self-driving cars are brought into the marketplace and there's not been serious attention to the car motion sickness issue, we'll have all of those first adopters that will be posting YouTube videos of them upchucking in that state-of-the-art fancy new self-driving car. Let's avoid that. I've already got a bumper sticker for my self-driving car, and it says "Anti-Motion Sickness On-Board for Your Comfort."

CHAPTER 3

RAIN DRIVING
FOR
SELF-DRIVING CARS

Lance B. Eliot

'

CHAPTER 3
RAIN DRIVING FOR SELF-DRIVING CARS

There is an ongoing joke among Southern California drivers that when the rain comes along we freak out and don't know what to do (this might be as much a local joke as it is an East Coast view of those "crazy" drivers on0 the West Coast). With just a few drops of rain, traffic seems to become snarled, even more so than normal. Drivers don't know whether to hit the brakes or hit the accelerator. And, because traffic is delayed, it causes some drivers to speed-up as a means to try and mitigate the fact that they've been slowed down – all of which then contributes to fear of heightened fender benders and the traffic getting even more bogged down. It's a viscous driving cycle during the rain.

Fortunately, we only get about 15 inches of rain annually, which is not much in comparison to the whopping 40+ inches that a New York City or Seattle would get. Nonetheless, the relative scarcity of rain does perhaps make us less prepared for the rain. Less preparation includes that we don't have working windshield wiper blades, or we are driving on bare tires. Less preparation also includes a forgotten understanding of how to drive safely in rainy conditions.

Those little droplets of rain can be a nuisance. Many assume that rain droplets are teardrop shaped, but the reality is that they are more akin to the shape of a parachute for larger sized droplets, and they are the shape of a hamburger bun for smaller sized droplets. Besides the size of the raindrops, another factor while driving is the amount of drops, and the intensity as they are coming down from the skies, plus their duration. A very brief rain shower with a few lazy, miniature drops is usually easier to manage than a downpour of a lengthy period with drops that seem as big as grapes.

Rain can certainly be more than just a nuisance. According to the National Highway Traffic Safety Administration (NHTSA), rain conditions account for nearly half (about 46%) of all weather-related accidents in the United States. In comparison, snow encompassed about one-firth (17%) of weather-related accidents. Now, this is a somewhat questionable comparison in that it is likely that less drivers get on the roads when it snows, while with rain there are a lot more drivers, and so we would anticipate that there would be a higher volume of accidents.

I think we can all agree that rain presents added difficulties when driving a car. The road gets wet, and provides a more dangerous surface upon which to drive. The car gets wet, mainly of which can obscure the vision of the driver. When you have lots of cars all driving in the rain, you get a smorgasbord of wet surfaces and a myriad of rain-savvy and rain-confused drivers that can or cannot readily see what they are doing. Even if you are professional rain driver, if we put you into the middle of traffic with a lot of panicky rain drivers, you are unlikely to come out of it unscathed.

What does this have to do with AI self-driving cars?

At the Cybernetic Self-Driving Car Institute, we are advancing the capability of AI to appropriately drive a self-driving car in rainy conditions.

Today, most of the self-driving cars aren't yet able to drive proficiently in the rain. In fact, when you see a slick video of a self-driving car that seems to be zooming along, you'll often notice that it is not doing so in rainy conditions. Instead, often the road is dry and there's not a rain cloud in the sky. Given the widespread aspect of rain, being common in much of the country for a substantial part of the year, we definitely need self-driving cars that can properly and appropriate drive in the rain.

For Level 5 true self-driving cars, which are self-driving cars that are supposed to be able to drive in the same manner as a human driver, we are expecting that the AI will be able to drive the car according to the aspects of the rainy circumstance. For Level 4 self-driving cars, the AI is not expected to necessarily be able to drive in the rain, or it can at least try to drive in the rain and if it somehow gets to a point where it can't further do so, it will hand control over to a human driver in the car.

This handing over protocol can be dangerous, since suppose that the self-driving car has gotten itself into a pickle of a really bad rain and might be nearing a skidding situation and be veering out-of-control. Simply handing the controls over to a human is not a cure-all. The human might not have sufficient time to overcome the situation, or might not have any options left as to how to get out of the predicament.

What makes things so hard to drive a self-driving car in the rain?

Let's consider the various facets that come along with rain related driving.

Roadway Surface

The roadway can become very slippery when wet. This means that the tires of the car might not grip the road well. The AI needs to be able to realize that the roads are wet, and determine how to best maneuver during turns, or how to best proceed from a standing still position to a moving state, and so on. If the AI tries to accelerate in the same manner as on a dry surface, the odds are that the wheels will spin or the car will skid, all of which can lead to a dangerous situation for the self-driving car and its occupants (and other cars, and pedestrians, etc.).

Hydroplaning

I'm sure you all remember in your high school classes on driving that you need to watch out for hydroplaning. This is the circumstance of a layer of water that sits between your tires and the road. Thus, you can end-up sitting on top of the water and not actually directly have the tires on the road itself. When this happens, your control of the car is greatly diminished. We have the AI prepared for this situation, and once it detects that hydroplaning is underway, it enacts a hydroplaning mode involving reducing acceleration, steering in the direction of the hydroplaning, and avoids slamming on the brakes. The AI also has to know what's nearby the car and how much room it has to gain control of the self-driving car without ramming into others or other objects.

Standing Water

There are sensors on the self-driving car that are looking at the roadway and scanning for standing water. As you know, a puddle can be either fun and safe to splash through, or it might be hiding a pothole that can damage your car and toss the steering into turmoil. Detecting standing water is harder than you might think, due to not only determining where the water is, but also trying to gauge how deep it is. The AI also needs to be considering options such as avoiding standing water, perhaps changing lanes or otherwise making a safe maneuver to avoid getting into the water moat.

Crown or Center Driving

During rain, the AI tries to keep the self-driving car toward the crown or center of the roadway. This is due to the aspect that most roadways are designed with a bit of a bow, allowing water to more easily drain off the road. You often see lots of deep water next to the sides of the road, which is partially because the water is draining to that position. The AI tries to keep the self-driving car away from the sides of the road, if feasible. This cannot be a hard-and-fast rule, since there are driving situations whereby the side of the road is the safer alternative and thus it is situational dependent.

Rain Driving Mode

As much as feasible, the AI tries to go slower than normal when navigating in the rain. A general rule-of-thumb is that speeds should be reduced by about one-third of the norm, such that if the speed normally is 55 miles per hour on a roadway then it is prudent to aim for 40 miles per hour, assuming that's even a safe speed in the circumstances. Likewise, distances between cars should be extended from the norm, allowing at least one-third more time or distance than usual. The AI also needs to make sure that the headlights are on, which aids not only the sensors of the self-driving car but also to warn other drivers and pedestrians about the presence of the self-driving car.

Car Readiness Condition for Rain

When someone wants a self-driving car to drive in the rain, as much as possible the AI needs to ascertain whether the self-driving car is ready for rain related driving. It can detect the tire pressure as one means of readiness. For some future cars there will be a means to detect the amount of tread on the tire (a bald tire is worse in the rain). The AI can also run through diagnostics of the sensors to determine that they are working, and also see if they are obscured by the rain. As an aside, you might find of interest that there are now some companies that are making special windshield wipers or other means to try and keep the sensors on a self-driving car free of rain, dust, dirt, snow, etc.

Driving Route

The AI of the self-driving car needs to consider the route carefully of wherever the self-driving car has been commanded to go. As a result of rain, there are often alternative routes that might avoid getting into areas that are flooded. Thus, the normal least-distance or fastest-time routes might not be viable anymore. I've had this happen to me many times, wherein I took my normal route on a rainy day, and found that this one road that dips low seems to get flooded right away, and I've had to backtrack to find another path, all of which made the drive much longer than if I had gone another way to start with.

Car Controls Usage

The AI needs to be aware of and be able to use the other automation on the car, such as the traction control feature, the anti-skid feature, and the anti-locking brake system (ABS). Those features are going to be pretty much standard on all cars, including self-driving cars. Those features are used by human drivers, and likewise the AI needs to know how to drive the car and consider those features too. Some assume that those features will have the AI embedded into them, but this is not likely the case right away. Instead, they will be the conventional standalone capabilities and it is up to the AI to drive the car with the realization that it can use those features during the driving task.

Sensors

Probably one of the biggest concerns for a self-driving car will be the sensors. Are the sensors going to be able to contend with rain?

We all know that a camera has troubles when it rains. The lens becomes obscured by the rain. Images can be distorted. We cannot necessarily see as far as we could in a dry situation. Indeed, as mentioned, there are third-party companies now coming to market with specialized aspects that help to keep the camera lens clear. This ranges from innovations such as miniature windshield wipers to heat-related mechanisms to get the water off the camera.

No matter what you do though to keep the cameras able to be clear, the odds are that you'll still end-up with problems due to the rain. As such, the AI needs to deal with the images that are going to be partial or cloudy or whatever. In addition, the AI might need to rely on some of the other sensory devices more so in the rain, and be less able to use the cameras. It is important that neural networks trained to inspect images are also trained to deal with images that are rain related (some datasets don't have rain related images, and so the neural networks have not been able to get trained on finding features in those kinds of images).

LIDAR, which is a type of laser that acts like radar, often is a key sensory device on most self-driving cars. There has been quite a lot of study about how rain impacts LIDAR. On the one hand, you would assume that something emitting laser beams is going to have troubles with the rain. Rain droplets are small but can be very efficient at reflections, and so can potentially create false readings. Studies show that there are ways around this.

For example, statistically a raindrop should not be in the same spot for very long, since it is falling, and thus if the LIDAR spots something that appears and disappears, the odds are that it is a raindrop in that circumstance. Also, raindrops tend to divert the signal toward the ground, and so by also looking at the ground plane it is possible to figure out what the rain is doing to the signals. Generally, research seems to show that LIDAR intensity decreases as the rain increases. Anyway, however it comes out, there are definitely issues to be dealt with when in the rain, and further advances in LIDAR will be needed to improve performance in the rain (including making sure the emitter surface does not get obscured by droplets).

Mixing With Human Drivers

Let's not forget that the self-driving car will be driving around in the same places as human driven cars. I know that some believe in a utopia, where the world will be only self-driving cars, but that's not in the cards for a very long time, if ever. So, the AI needs to realize that the other cars on the roadway are being driven in some cases by other AI, while in some cases by human drivers. The AI needs to be wary of those human drivers that are driving overly fast or overly slow, and drivers that suddenly swerve to avoid a puddle, and drivers that do the craziest things while driving in the rain.

Traffic Navigation

The AI for rain conditions will try to keep from getting boxed-in by other cars. In other words, while on a freeway, having cars in front of, behind, to the left, to the right, and immediately all around the self-driving car means that the AI has few options for maneuvering in the rain. It needs to try and keep options open as much as possible. This takes some really good driving skills. Changing lanes can be much harder in the rain, and requires more careful action. Driving behind trucks is not advised as the trucks toss-up a lot of water from the roadway. These are all parts of the AI's capability for rain related driving.

Interaction With Occupants

Another aspect for the AI will be interacting with the occupants of the self-driving car. Humans that are in the car will likely want to know how the self-driving car is doing. Why did it take a left when normally the way to get to the destination is to the right? Also, if the AI determines the driving situation is extremely dangerous, it should interact with the occupants to let them know, and possibly offer options such as safely getting off the roadway and finding a place to stop, hopefully waiting to let the rain subside.

Conclusion

As you can see, there's a lot involved in having the AI of the self-driving car contend with rain related driving. It's not so easy. That's why many of the self-driving cars aren't yet able to drive in the rain. Some that can drive in the rain are very limited in the rain related conditions that they can succeed in. For example, if it is pouring rain and the rain has been going for a while, and the roads are flooded, this can exceed what the AI is able to deal with.

All of the aspects of the core components of a self-driving car are impacted by the rain, including:

- Sensors – sensors might not work, might work differently in the rain
- Sensor Fusion – might need to rely on some sensors more than others in the rain
- Virtual World Model – might be difficult to keep the world model in full shape due to rain
- Action Planning – might need to adjust action plans beyond normal driving due to rain
- Controls Activation – might need to use the accelerator, brakes, steering in different ways
- Tactical AI – must be aware of the rain conditions and rain-related driving mode
- Strategic AI – must be aware of the overarching use of the car when in rain
- Self-Aware AI – must be aware of what the car is able to do when it is in the rain

When you see a novice driver such as a teenager driving in the rain, you can see how scared they can get. For very good reasons. Driving in the rain is not the same as driving in non-rain non-wet conditions. This is an arduous task for a self-driving car to take on, but it is a "must" since ultimately self-driving cars aren't going to be considered much of a success if they have to sit out the rain. Nobody wants a scaredy cat AI self-driving car that refuses to leave the garage when there's rain outside.

CHAPTER 4
EDGE COMPUTING
FOR
SELF-DRIVING CARS

CHAPTER 4
EDGE COMPUTING
FOR
SELF-DRIVING CARS

During the Cold War era, the Soviet military doctrine was one of strict control by the central Soviet command. All decisions about the use of military force had to be first approved by Soviet commanders at the highest levels of the hierarchy, and there was little if any latitude afforded to local commanders. With a massive military force consisting of over 53,000 tanks, 4,900 aircraft, and some 360 submarines, the Soviet top authorities wanted to make any and all decisions regarding military actions. You might think that this seems like a very prudent policy, since it would presumably prevent local commanders from taking rogue actions.

The counter-argument to this approach was that it meant that the Soviet ability to act quickly was substantively degraded. Local commanders that might be aware of a local situation brewing were obligated to report up the chain to the top command, and then had to wait to take any action until specifically authorized to do so. In contrast, the American military allowed for some autonomy by its local commanders, meaning that the USA forces could potentially be nimbler and quickly act or react to an emerging situation.

If you've ever seen the movie "Crimson Tide," you might recall that a crucial scene in the movie (spoiler alert!) involves the USS Alabama nuclear submarine and the dynamic tension between the Captain and the XO of the ship. A message had come via radio from the Naval command that the sub should go ahead and arm its nuclear missiles and fire them within a set time frame. But, a second message then comes to the sub, and the message is only partially received. Should they proceed based on the first message which was entirely received and very clear cut, or should they perhaps not proceed since the second message was inadvertently cut-off and could have been an order to desist and not fire the nuclear missiles. The Captain and the XO get into quite an argument about what they should do.

Decisions at a local level can have life-or-death consequences.

How does this relate to AI self-driving cars?

At the Cybernetic Self-Driving Car Institute, we are advancing the use of edge computing for AI self-driving cars. Edge computing is a relatively newer term and has become increasingly important as the era of the Internet of Things (IoT) has begun blossoming.

Edge computing is the idea and approach that sometimes the computer processing and algorithmic decisions need to occur at the extreme edge of a computer network. Rather than having processing and algorithmic decisions being made in the cloud, the notion is to push the intelligence and computing closer to the action. This allows for immediacy of analysis.

Imagine if you have a factory that is being run by all sorts of automated pumps and turbines. If the equipment is connected to the cloud, and if all of the data coming off those devices goes up into the cloud, it would be tempting to also have the cloud actually controlling those devices. When a pump needs to be turned-off, a command issued from the cloud, through a network, and down to the pump would tell it to switch off. When a pump is having troubles, it would send a message through the network and up into the cloud. This would be a centralized way of managing the equipment.

Suppose though that the pump begins to have a problem and it takes a bit of time for it to communicate through the network, and then for the network to convey the message to the cloud, and then there's time that the cloud application needs to process the information, and then issue a command, which goes through the network, and finally reaches to the pump. It could be that the pump by then has gone completely haywire. The delay in the steps from pump-cloud-pump might have taken so long that the cloud missed the chance to save the pump.

With the advent of the Internet of Things (IoT), this kind of consideration is going to become increasingly prominent and important. The Gartner Group, an IT research firm, estimates that there were 8.4 billion IoT devices in 2017, and by the year 2020 there will be 20.4 billion IoT devices in use. Those IoT devices will need to communicate with the cloud, and the cloud itself might become increasingly bogged with traffic, thus, adding further to delays between the cloud and the IoT devices communicating with the cloud.

Any IoT devices that have life-or-death consequences, such as medical IoT devices in the home, could put humans at risk.

This could also be said of self-driving cars. Self-driving cars have lots of sensory devices on them, including cameras, LIDAR for laser or light radar use, sonar devices, and so on. Many of the self-driving car makers are envisioning that the data from the sensors will flow up into the cloud that the auto maker has setup for their self-driving cars. This allows the auto makers to collect tons of driving data and be able to use machine learning to improve AI self-driving practices.

The question arises as to how much of the processing should take place at the "edge," which in this case is the self-driving car and its myriad local devices, versus taking place in the cloud.

For practical reasons, we already know that much of the processing has to occur at the edge, since the speed by which the sensory data needs to be analyzed is bound by the fact that the self-driving car is in motion and needs timely indications of what is around the car. Estimates suggest that a self-driving car that runs eight hours a day (which is a fraction of what is ultimately expected, i.e., we assume that eventually they will be operating 24 hours per day), would produce at least 40TB of data (according to Intel). That's a lot of data to be transmitting back-and-forth over a network.

Estimates also suggest that sending data back-and-forth across a network would take at least 150-200 milliseconds, assuming that there is a strong network connection and that the connection remains continuous for the time to make the transmission. That's actually a huge amount of time, given that the car is in motion and that rapid decisions need to be made about the control of the car. In some respects, if the cloud is calling the shots, it is like the Soviet military doctrine and would likely cause delays, perhaps life-or-death delays.

Therefore, self-driving cars need to make use of edge computing. This involves having enough localized computational processing capability and memory capacity to be able to ensure that the self-driving car and the AI are able to perform their needed tasks. You might be saying that we should just go ahead and put lots and lots of processors and memory on-board the self-driving cars. That's a nice idea, but keep in mind that you are going to be adding a lot of cost to the self-driving car, plus adding equipment that will eventually be breaking down and need maintenance, and that requires power to run, and adds weight to the car, etc.

So, we need to be thoughtful and judicious as to how much localized processing needs to be done. Keep in mind too that it is not necessarily a mutually exclusive proposition of local versus cloud. A well-designed AI self-driving car will be able to mix together the localized processing and the cloud processing.

For example, the self-driving car might be processing the sensory data in real-time and taking driving actions accordingly. Meanwhile, it is sending the data up to the cloud. The cloud processes the data, looking for longer-term patterns, and eventually sends down to the self-driving car some updates as based on doing an analysis of the data. In this case, we've split the effort into two parts, one that is doing the life-or-death rapid processing at the local (edge) level, and the more overview oriented efforts at the cloud level that aren't particular time sensitive in nature.

The ability to push data up to the cloud and get back results will be dependent upon:

- Communication devices on the self-driving car
- Latency involved in communicating via a network
- Bandwidth of a network
- Availability of a network
- Reliability of a network
- Communication within the self-driving car

Notice that this depends on the nature of the network and network connection that the self-driving car has established for use. When you think about your network at home and how it at times has hiccups and delays, it is a bit disconcerting to think that the network of the self-driving car might also be based on the Internet and the vagaries that go along with that kind of network. This is why it makes sense to not base the self-driving car real-time efforts on the cloud per se.

There are some devices on the self-driving car that would be considered edge-dedicated, meaning that they are completely reliant on their own local efforts. They don't care about the cloud. Though data they collect might be sent up to the cloud, they aren't dependent upon anything coming back from the cloud. There are edge-shared devices that are able to split efforts with the cloud, undertaking some tasks entirely locally and other tasks in a joint collaborative manner with the cloud.

Doing image analysis on pictures streaming in from a camera on the front right bumper of the self-driving car is something likely best done at the edge. The image analyzer on-board the processors of the self-driving car would be looking for indications of other cars, motorcycles, pedestrians, and so on. This is then fed into the sensor fusion, bringing together the sensory analyses coming from the LIDAR, radar, etc. The sensor fusion is being fed into a virtual world model of the surrounding driving scene. All of this is being undertaken at the edge (in the self-driving car).

The AI of the self-driving car is running on local processors in the self-driving car, and interprets the virtual world model to decide what actions to take with the car. And, the AI then commands the car controls to accelerate or brake, and steers the car. We would anticipate that by-and-large this all takes place at the edge.

Here's how it looks:
- Sensor data collection at the edge
- Sensor fusion at the edge
- Virtual world model update at the edge
- AI action plan determined at the edge
- AI issues car-control commands at the edge
- Self-driving executes the car-control commands at the edge

We could instead include the cloud as a non-real-time collaborator, meaning that the cloud would be kept apprised of what's happening, but would not be undertaking control related to the self-driving car:
- Sensor data collection at the edge
- Send data up to the cloud, but don't wait for the cloud
- Sensor fusion at the edge
- Send sensor fusion result up to the cloud, but don't wait for the cloud
- Virtual world model update at the edge
- Send virtual world model up to the cloud, but don't wait for the cloud
- AI action plan determined at the edge
- Send AI action plan up to the cloud, but don't wait for the cloud
- AI issues car control commands at the edge
- Send AI-issued car control commands up to the cloud, but don't wait for the cloud
- Self-driving car controls executive the commands
- Get updates from the cloud and update the edge when feasible

We've interlaced the transmitting of the edge information up to the cloud. This could also be done instead at say the end of the above loop, rather than trying to interlace it.

If you were to decide to put the cloud control into these steps, here's how it might look:

- Sensor data collection at the edge
- Send data up to the cloud, wait for the cloud
- Sensor fusion at the cloud
- Virtual world model update at the cloud
- AI action plan determined at the cloud
- AI issues car control commands via the cloud
- Wait until the cloud car-control commands are received
- Self-driving car executes the car-control commands

In this above edge-cloud model, the self-driving car is pretty much a "dumb" car and not doing much of any real processing on its own. As previously mentioned, the concern here is whether or not the communication would be reliable enough and consistent and fast enough for what needs to be done. The cloud itself might have some of the fastest computers on earth, but in the end it is the network communication that could undermine that hefty processing power.

One of the values of using the cloud would be the ability to leverage the much larger processing and memory capacity that we could have in the cloud versus what we've got loaded onto the self-driving car. For example, when I mentioned that doing image analysis from pictures streaming in is best done at the edge, it could be that there is a massive scale learning-in-the-cloud capability that has thousands upon thousands of images from thousands upon thousands of self-driving cars, and it might be able to do a better job of image analysis than some smaller neural network sitting on a processor at the edge.

Thus, well-designed self-driving cars are able to have the autonomy needed at the edge, and also leverage the cloud when appropriate. We might for example have the self-driving car AI get updates from the cloud when the self-driving car is available to do so, such as maybe when the car is parked and otherwise not being used. It could enhance a local edge-based neural network, doing so via leveraging the larger-scale neural network learnings from the cloud.

There are some that believe we also need fog computing.

Fog computing is the middle-ground between edge computing and cloud computing. We might have intermediary computing that acts as a go-between for the edge and the cloud. This might mean that we'd have computer servers setup along the roadways, and those systems could much more quickly and reliably communicate with self-driving cars that are whizzing along on the highway than would the cloud per se. Thus, you get presumably a cloud-like capability that won't have the same kinds of latency and issues as the true cloud. This requires adding a lot of infrastructure, which would tend to be costly at both initial setup and keeping it maintained.

In the fog model, you have edge-fog-cloud as the elements involved, rather than just edge-cloud. Some are doubtful about the fog approach, and though the name itself is kind of clever, some also say that the name won't catch-on (since the word "fog" seems to have a bad connotation). The jury is still out about fog computing.

Developers of self-driving cars are finding that they need to carefully consider how edge computing is best arranged for self-driving cars. This will be an evolving innovation and we are likely to see the AI self-driving car first-generation, we'll call it 1.0, gradually become version 2.0, making self-driving cars better able to be both standalone as needed and yet also leverage the cloud as needed.

CHAPTER 5
MOTORCYCLES
AS
SELF-DRIVING VEHICLES

Lance B. Eliot

CHAPTER 5

MOTORCYCLES AS
SELF-DRIVING VEHICLES

When I was in my late-teens, I wanted to ride motorcycles. It was considered cool, and still is by many. There was this maverick image of being a motorcycle rider. You were free. You went with the wind. You were different. You were someone that bucked the system. I admit too that the imagery also suggested that I could get girls by being a motorcycle rider (that was a big influencer in my teens!).

A good friend of mine was a dirt bike rider and he offered to show me how to drive a motorcycle.

Notice that I just used the word "drive" when mentioning a motorcycle. There are motorcyclists that don't like the use of the word drive when referring to being on a motorcycle. They say that you "drive a car" but that for a motorcycle you "ride a motorcycle." I certainly don't want to quibble on this point, but I would say that when you "ride" on something it could be that you are merely a passenger, while when you "drive" something it implies you are actually directing the activities of the machine. This will be an important distinction here, and so that's why I bring up the semantics aspects of the words "drive" versus "ride."

Anyway, my parents were dead set against my riding and/or driving on motorcycles. They felt strongly that a motorcycle was a dangerous form of transportation. They emphasized that those on the motorcycle could easily be thrown off the motorcycle and therefore could then be vulnerable to being run over by cars or that your body would certainly get torn apart if you hit the pavement at say 60 miles per hour. They also pointed out that there are a lot of car drivers that don't pay attention to motorcycles and thus even if I was really good at motorcycle riding or driving that nonetheless a car at any time could plow into me. They showed me pictures of people that had been involved in motorcycle accidents and deaths (these were rather daunting photos to look at), along with sharing with me the sobering statistics depicting the number of motorcycle incidents annually (a chilling number).

This was a quite rational way of explaining why I should neither ride on and nor drive a motorcycle. So, of course, being a teenager, I completely disregarded their advice and sneaked out to the desert with my friend so that I could learn how to drive a motorcycle. Yes, that's the maverick in me.

In the end, I never personally took to motorcycles that much. I would go riding with my friend in the desert, but never pursued getting a motorcycle license and did not drive a motorcycle on city streets. It was a fun thing to do on special occasions when we went out to the desert. That was about it for me in terms of my particular interest in motorcycles. Each to their own cup of tea.

Well, I am now quite interested in motorcycles, though for a different reason than I once was. Nowadays, I am interested in motorcycles because of their potential for being self-driving vehicles.

What's that, you ask, a motorcycle that is a self-driving vehicle? Huh?

When I bring up the topic of self-driving motorcycles at my various presentations on driverless cars and autonomous vehicles, I usually get some pretty quizzical looks. People will often say to me that it makes no sense to have a self-driving motorcycle. In their view, the whole purpose of a motorcycle is that it involves the close relationship between the human rider (driver) and the bike itself. A motorcycle is intended to provide that freedom of driving that allows the maverick to go where they want and how they want. This seems completely antithetical to the concept of having a self-driving capability.

I know that it might seem like an odd combination. Motorcycle and AI combined together to have a self-driving motorcycle. Where does the human fit into that equation, you might wonder. In a sense, you could look at this combination in a different light and see that if you did have a self-driving motorcycle that it could open the door toward more potential humans riding on motorcycles than we have today.

Yes, when you consider that driving a motorcycle does require a sufficient skillset and you technically do need to get a motorcycle driving license, there is a bit of a barrier to entry of deciding you want to be a motorcycle driver. Even if you are a motorcycle driver today and think that the getting of a driver's license is a bit of a joke (some would say it is extremely easy), it is indeed a perceived barrier to a lot of people that have contemplated getting a motorcycle. Also, the mechanical aspects of using a motorcycle just seems overly complicated to many in terms of how to use the clutch, how to use the throttle, etc.

Voila, imagine if there was a self-driving motorcycle that all a human needed to do was sit on the motorcycle and the rest of the driving was done by the on-board AI. No driver's license needed for the human. No awareness of how to start, drive, or stop the motorcycle is needed by the human. Just jump on the motorcycle and away you go -- I assure you that this would attract a whole lot of people that otherwise would not have ventured onto a motorcycle. It could blast wide open the sales of motorcycles.

You might find of interest that the current market for motorcycles in the United States is somewhat in the doldrums. Sales have been flat and tend to be falling. Baby boomers are aging out of the motorcycle industry. Millennials aren't as attracted to motorcycles as were the baby boomers. Most of the buyers of motorcycles continue to be predominantly men. Generally, few women, and few minorities, are buying and using motorcycles. If you are a motorcycle dealer, it is rough times, for sure, and right now the future looks gloomy.

In fact, the future looks downright ugly. There are many pundits that are predicting an utter meltdown in the motorcycle industry once the self-driving car comes along. The thinking is that people will not care anymore about using motorcycles and will be very happy to just ride along in self-driving cars. And, there are some that predict we will change the nature of our roads to accommodate self-driving cars, making special lanes for them and ultimately forcing human driven cars into slow lanes to discourage humans from driving cars. Likewise, they claim that motorcycles won't be allowed around the self-driving cars since a human driven motorcyclist will mess up the coordinated dance of self-driving cars that are trying to make traffic flow maximally efficient.

There was even a recent accident in San Francisco involving a human driven motorcycle and a self-driving car – so far, the motorcyclist was considered at fault. Supposedly, the motorcyclist made a lane change and the motorcycle and the self-driving car bumped into each other -- the police faulted the motorcyclist for not making a safe lane change. This kind of circumstance will likely give rise to self-driving car proponents including politicians of seeking some kind of ban of motorcycles on the roadways that have self-driving cars.

Now, I don't necessarily agree that we'll as a society be entirely ban human motorcyclists to a second-class citizen position on our highways, and nor do I see that the motorcycle messes up the traffic smarts of self-driving cars per se (in my view, the self-driving cars should be AI savvy enough to deal with this and not place the burden onto the shoulders of the motorcyclists).

I can imagine that with the safety and security of self-driving cars that there will be a segment of society that becomes emboldened to seek out adventure. Self-driving motorcycles could be that outlet of adventure. Just as being an occupant in a self-driving car won't take any skill by a human, nor would the human need to have any true skill in riding on a self-driving motorcycle. In theory, it would be like sitting on a motorcycle behind a top pro motorcycle driver, and just hanging on and enjoying the ride.

This does bring up one big question that I know you motorcycle driving fans have. Will a self-driving motorcycle allow the human rider to drive the motorcycle, or will the motorcycle be only driven by the AI?

For those that aren't into motorcycles, you might think this question is not important, and your view might be that of course we wouldn't let the humans drive the motorcycles any longer. Certainly, it would be better and safer to always have the AI driving the motorcycles. The humans would be occupants, that's it. All I can say to that thinking is that we are going to have some motorcyclists that will tell you that you will only pry their "cold dead hands" from the throttle of their motorcycle and that never shall it be that humans cannot actually drive a motorcycle.

Let's put to the side for now the debate about whether humans will be allowed to drive a motorcycle, and just for now focus on the topic of self-driving motorcycles overall.

A self-driving motorcycle would allow for a human passenger or passengers to glide along and enjoy the wind and freedom of being on a motorcycle. The humans would not need to know how to drive the motorcycle. Presumably, they would not do any of the controls. The humans would not steer, nor brake, nor accelerate. The human is strictly a rider.

The human though does need to actively participate in the riding process per se. Of course, the human rider would need to lean properly into the riding process for the physics of the ride, and would need to make sure they stay on the motorcycle. In other words, the human does have some duties, but the duties are all about being a good passenger. This doesn't require much of any skill and is really just more about doing the right thing when on the motorcycle.

You could somewhat say the same thing about being an occupant in a self-driving car, in that you are expected to not roll down the windows of the self-driving car and climb out on the hood of the self-driving car, namely, there are proper things to do when being a passenger in a self-driving car and likewise for a self-driving motorcycle.

Some of you might be wondering whether the human occupant would have to be on the motorcycle in order to keep the motorcycle balanced while it is being driven by the AI. In essence, would it be a requirement that a self-driving motorcycle could only move along if there was a human passenger. The answer is no. I say this because Honda has developed a new concept motorcycle that can balance itself, doing so not only at regular speeds but also at a low-speed crawl and even when the motorcycle comes to a complete stop. So, interestingly, we could have motorcycles that drive along our roads all by themselves. No human needed. Admittedly, this would be at first a bit eerie. Though, keep in mind that we are going to have self-driving cars that drive around all by themselves and there won't necessarily be any human passengers in them either. It's a new reality.

The envisioned future of self-driving cars is that your AI self-driving car will be able to drive on its own here-and-there as based on the needs of the human owner; for example, it takes you to work, and then maybe you opt to send your self-driving car home where it can then be used by the kids to get over to school, and later in the day your self-driving car picks them up after school and drops them back at home, and finally at the end of the workday it comes to pick you up. All the time, the self-driving car is without any human driver, and for some of the time there isn't any humans inside the self-driving car at all.

You could do the same with a self-driving motorcycle. Maybe ride it to work, and then send it on its own over to a friend that needs to use it for some errands, and then the friend routes it back over to your office.

Some of the motorcycle-futurists envision that a motorcycle might be redesigned as a result of the self-driving capability. For example, one concept is the Exocycle, which is a self-driving motorcycle that looks somewhat like the ones used in the movie Tron. It is an enclosed cockpit like contraption. The human occupants sit inside of a frame and are protected from the environment similar to sitting inside a car. A distinction for the Exocycle over a self-driving car is that the

Exocycle remains relatively slim in comparison to a self-driving car. That being the case, the designers also came up with the idea that two Exocycles could connect to each other, side-by-side, and drive together, doing so in a width that is somewhat the same as the width of a car.

It seems doubtful that the Exocycle would give the same kind of thrill ride that a conventionally shaped motorcycle would provide. As such, I think that the concept of an enclosed self-driving motorcycle is perhaps closer to a self-driving car concept than it is akin to a self-driving motorcycle per se.

BMW has a futuristic concept motorcycle called the Motorrad Vision Next 100, which pretty much resembles a Speed Racer look-and-feel. They suggest that the design eliminates the need for the rider of the motorcycle to wear any protective gear (this seems somewhat questionable), but anyway the design of the Motorrad assumes that the rider is the driver, and so it is not envisioned as a self-driving motorcycle. If you are a believer that motorcycles will always (or should always) have a human driver, the BMW approach might be rather appealing to you.

An interesting alternative to a self-driving motorcycle consists of having a robot that can drive a motorcycle. This is clever because it means that all existing motorcycles could (in theory) become "self-driving" by simply having the robot sit on the motorcycle and drive it along. You could then sit behind the robot and hang-on as a passenger, or you could send your robot-driven motorcycle to go do errands for you.

Yamaha pitted an early version of such a robot against a professional motorcycle driver, and the company admits that trying to develop such a "humanoid" type robot is like a moonshot. I'd speculate that having a fully functional humanoid-like robot that could also drive a motorcycle is a lot further off in the future than the formulation of a self-driving motorcycle. But, anyway, it's an intriguing idea that posits the idea that rather than trying to reformulate the motorcycle itself, just create a human shaped robot that could drive a motorcycle.

Let's take a moment and consider what makes a self-driving motorcycle a difficult proposition.

First, when you look at a self-driving car, you'll notice that there are numerous sensors on the self-driving car. The added bulk of the sensors is not overwhelming and so a car can bear the added weight and such. For a motorcycle, putting those same kinds of sensors onto the slim frame of a motorcycle is not going to be easy, especially if we wanted to include multiple cameras, radar units, sonar units, LIDAR, etc. In that sense, one must question the viability of having a self-driving motorcycle simply due to where to put all the sensory devices, and yet at the same time keep the motorcycle slim and trim.

You would either need to accept the idea that the shape and size of a motorcycle will need to blossom quite a bit, or, perhaps the sensors themselves will gradually become more miniaturized. Fortunately, the tech industry is continually trying to reduce the size of such sensory devices and that bodes well for the self-driving motorcycle.

Next aspect to keep in mind is that there is a lot of computer processing needed to undertake the AI part of the self-driving vehicle. Once again, for a self-driving car, we can hide the computers in the underbody and in the trunk, and so it doesn't particularly bulk-up the size of a car. For a motorcycle, we are once again faced with the sizing aspects of a slim and trim bike, and the question arises as to where we'll fit the computer gear needed to sustain the self-driving capabilities.

There is also a significant cost factor involved in a self-driving vehicle. The sensor devices and the computer systems all add quite a bit to the cost of a self-driving vehicle. We tend to think of motorcycles as a less expensive alternative to cars, but a self-driving motorcycle could skyrocket in price due to all the added hardware and software. The same can be said of a self-driving car, though we are all pretty much used to seeing expensive cars on the road and so adding another chunk of cost might not be as bad for the self-driving car buyer as it would for the self-driving motorcycle buyer.

Hopefully, the costs of the hardware and software for a self-driving vehicle will gradually come down, which makes sense as the technology becomes more commoditized and as the volume of such vehicles rises in the marketplace.

There are ways in which a self-driving motorcycle needs perhaps more sophisticated capabilities than does a self-driving car, and this will make it harder to develop a true self-driving motorcycle.

A self-driving car would usually be abiding by the lanes of the roadway and stay within a lane. Indeed, most self-driving cars do a rather simple process of lane following, which is achieved by scanning for the lane painted on the road and following it along. Lane changes by a self-driving car are intended to take place only when needed and it is not an especially continuous practice.

For the self-driving motorcycle, we can assume that the motorcyclists will want to do what human drivers do, such as lane splitting. This is a harder problem than what the self-driving car faces. Also, a motorcycle can go places that a conventional car cannot readily go, such as in narrow spaces or even off the roadway and onto other areas. This again ups the ante in terms of the needed sophistication of the AI for the self-driving motorcycle.

This brings up an ethics related question that somewhat confronts self-driving cars, but perhaps even more so for self-driving motorcycles. Namely, should a self-driving motorcycle be able to undertake either illegal maneuvers or at least even ill-advised maneuvers? Or, should the AI be shaped in such a means that it won't allow for any kind of ill-advised driving and nor any illegal driving. For existing human drivers of motorcycles, I am guessing that if a self-driving motorcycle has severe restrictions to keep it legal and not allow ill-advised driving, some of the value and joy of motorcycle riding will be driven out of the self-driving motorcycle for those human riders.

Would a self-driving motorcycle be allowed to exceed the speed limit? Would a self-driving motorcycle be allowed to do a street race against another self-driving motorcycle? Could you "burn rubber" with a self-driving motorcycle? These are all questions that aren't technological, since any of those aspects could be undertaken by the AI, and instead fall into the realm of societal and political dimensions.

Other interesting aspects of a self-driving motorcycles also arise that aren't necessarily raised with self-driving cars. For example, suppose a self-driving motorcycle comes up to a red light at an intersection and properly comes to a stop. It has been sent on an errand by its owner and there is no human riding on the motorcycle. Meanwhile, while stopped at the red light, a pedestrian decides to run over and hop onto the self-driving motorcycle. What happens now? Should the self-driving motorcycle proceed along and allow for the interloper to join for a free ride? Presumably, we wouldn't want that. So, somehow the self-driving motorcycles needs to be able to sense the presence of a rider, and also then determine what to do when a stranger decides to jump on.

Another similar kind of question involves a self-driving motorcycle that has a human rider and suppose the human rider falls off the bike. Then what? Should the self-driving motorcycle come to a halt? Suppose though that the halting action takes the self-driving motorcycle some number of yards ahead to achieve. Would we expect the self-driving motorcycle to turn around and come back to where the human rider fell off?

I think you get the overall gist. There are going to be lots of situations involving self-driving motorcycles that differ from a self-driving car. Therefore, developing a self-driving motorcycle does not imply that we can simply port over the AI of a self-driving car and voila have ourselves a functional self-driving motorcycle. The particular aspects of a motorcycle will require a specialized AI capability. This then brings up an economic question – will there be enough money to be made from a self-driving motorcycle market to warrant the motorcycle makers or tech firms or auto makers to invest in developing self-driving motorcycles?

Some would say that the self-driving car will be sufficient and that fewer and fewer people will want or see the need for a self-driving motorcycle. There are others that say the self-driving car will gradually become so commonplace that there will be rising desire for something else, and that the "else" will be self-driving motorcycles. We'll see what happens as the future of the open road unwinds.

.

CHAPTER 6

CAPTCHA CYBER-HACKING AND SELF-DRIVING CARS

CHAPTER 6
CAPTCHA CYBER-HACKING
AND SELF-DRIVING CARS

You've likely had to enter a series of numbers and letters when accessing a web site that wanted "proof" that you are a human being and that you were not some kind of Internet bot. The typical approach involves your visual inspection of a grainy image that contains letters and numbers, and then having to try and figure out what those letters and numbers are. It is intentionally made difficult due to the aspect that the letters and numbers are usually smashed together, and they are often twisted and distorted so as to be hard to discern.

These challenge-response tests are known as CAPTCHA, which is an acronym for "Completely Automated Public Turing test to tell Computers and Humans Apart." The idea is that if a web site wants to keep automated bots from accessing their site, there needs to be some means to differentiate between whether a human is trying to access the web site or whether it is some kind of automation. Humans are quite good at visually being able to discern letters and numbers, and so the CAPTCHA aids in distinguishing whether the answerer is a human or a bot. Automated systems have a difficult time trying to ferret out amongst a twisted and distorted mix of letters and numbers the intended indication of what those distinct letters and numbers are.

Some people don't know why the CAPTCHA is being used and are pretty much just irritated by the whole thing. Why do I have to look at this stupid and obviously messed-up list of random letters and numbers, asks those that are not in-the-know. Makers of web sites are at times hesitant to use the CAPTCHA because it could dissuade people from using the web site and decrease the number of potential visitors to their site. But, those pesky automated bots that might otherwise become "false" visitors, meaning that the site might believe them to be actual humans, and also there are potential adverse aspects a bot might do at a web site, and so in the end it often is worthwhile to consider making use of CAPTCHA.

Now, you might be puzzled that the CAPTCHA is not readily able to be hacked by automation. One might assume that with the tremendous advances in Artificial Intelligence (AI) in recent times, certainly there must be a means to figure out those grainy images via automation. Well, it depends partially on how strong the CAPTCHA is. If the CAPTCHA makes use of a varied combination of letters and numbers that are really swerved and mushed together, along with varying the height and width of the characters, and if the number of such characters is sizable enough, the ability for an AI system to figure it out is quite limited today.

Of course, the worse it is for the AI also means that it is likely harder for the humans to figure out too. And, if it gets too hard for humans, you'll have neither bots and nor humans being able to pass the test. That's not very helpful in that it will simply prevent anyone or anything from succeeding – you might as well close down your web site since it won't be accessible at all.

To properly recognize the CAPTCHA, you need to perform at least three key visual and mental tasks:

- Recognition

You need to visually examine the image and recognize that there are letters and numbers in it. Any of the characters can be enlarged or shrunk in size, and can be at various angles. They can be stretched out or squeezed together. The parts of one character might be merged with the parts of another character. The number of variations is seemingly endless of how the CAPTCHA can obscure conventional letters and numbers. Humans seem to be able to relatively easily handle these invariant recognition aspects, namely that we can very quickly realize the essence of a letter or number shape, in spite of the distortions made to it.

- Segmentation

If I show you a letter or number and it is displayed on a standalone basis, such as the letter "h" and the letter "e," you have a much easier time generally of figuring it out. On the other hand, if I merge them with other letters and numbers, such as pushing together the "he" and making each flow into the other directly, it typically becomes harder to discern. The true shape of the letter or number becomes masked by its being merged with other letters and numbers. You need to be able to mentally disentangle the crammed together numbers and letters into a series of distinctive chunks, and within each chunk try to reconstruct what the individual letter or number might be.

- Contextual

By having multiple letters and numbers, you can often improve your odds of guessing any individual letter or number by considering the context of the characters within the overall image. That being said, many CAPTCHA's don't use regular words, since it would make things perhaps too easy to guess the individual characters. If the letters were "d" "o" "g" and you were able to guess the first two letters, it might be overly easy to guess the third letter. If instead the letters were "d" "g" "o" then you might not so readily be able to guess the entire set of letters because it does not make into a word that you would normally recognize.

There are numerous variations nowadays of CAPTCHA algorithms. Some use just letters and numbers, while some also add into the mix a variety of special characters such as an ampersand and a percentages symbol. You've likely also encountered CAPTCHA's that ask you to pick images that have something in common. For example, you are presented with six images of a grassy outdoor field, and are asked to mark the images that have a horse shown in the image. These aren't so easy because the horse will often be obscured or only a small portion of a horse appears in any given image.

The reason why the acronym of CAPTCHA mentions a Turing test is that there is a famous test in the field of AI that was proposed by the mathematician Alan Turing about how to determine whether an automated system could exhibit intelligence. The test consists of having a human ask questions or essentially interview another human and a separate AI system, for which the interviewer is not privy beforehand as to which is which, and if the interviewer is unable to tell the difference between the two interviewees, we presumably could declare that the automation has exhibited intelligent behavior. There are some that are critical of this test and don't believe it to be sufficient per se, but nonetheless it is quite famous and regarded by many as a key test for ascertaining AI.

In the case of CAPTCHA, the Turing test approach is being used to see if the human can outwit a bot that might be trying to also pass the same test. Whomever is able to figure out the letters and numbers is considered or assumed to be a human. Thus, if the bot can indeed figure out the CAPTCHA, it momentarily has won this kind of Turing test. I think we would all agree that even if some kind of automation can succeed in winning in a CAPTCHA contest, we would be hard pressed to say that it has exhibited human intelligence. In that sense, this is a small and extremely narrow version of a Turing test and not really what we all truly intend a Turing test to be able to achieve.

In fact, because the human is having to essentially prove they are a human by passing a CAPTCHA, some refer to this test as a Reverse Turing test. Here's why. The limelight of a conventional Turing test is for the automation to prove it has human-like capabilities. In this reverse Turing test, it is up to the human to prove that they are a human and able to perform better than the automation.

There is a popular CAPTCHA algorithm used as a plug-in for many WordPress developed web sites that is known as "Really Simple CAPTCHA." In a recent article about it, a developer showed how easy it can be to develop a simple AI system to be able to succeed at cracking the CAPTCHA challenges.

The CAPTCHA in this case consisted of a string of 4 characters that used a mixture of four fonts, and it avoided using the letters "o" and "i" to reduce any confusion by the humans that have to try and figure out the CAPTCHA generated images. Notice that by these limitations it becomes a much smaller problem to be solved, in the sense that rather than say using a string of 10 characters and using 25 fonts, and by eliminating some of the letters, the solution space is a lot smaller than otherwise.

The developer wanting to crack it used the popular Python programming language, along with the OpenCV set of programs that are freely available for doing image processing, and Keras which is a deep learning program written in Python. He also used TensorFlow, which is Google's machine learning library of programs (Keras uses TensorFlow). I mention the tools herein to be able to emphasize that the developer used off-the-shelf programming tools. He didn't need to resort to some "dark web" secretive code to be able to proceed to crack this CAPTCHA.

The CAPTCHA program was readily available as open source and therefore the developer could inspect the code at will. He then used the CAPTCHA to generate numerous samples of CAPTCHA images, doing so to create a set of training data. The training data consisted of each generated image and its right answer. This could then allow a pattern-matching system such as an artificial neural network to compare each image to the right answer, and then try to statistically figure out a pattern for being able to go from the seemingly inscrutable image to the desired answer.

After doing some transformations on the images, the developer fed the images into a neural network that he setup with two convolutional layers and with two hidden connected layers. According to his article, by just having ten passes through the training data set, the neural network was able to achieve full accuracy. He then tried it with actual new CAPTCHA generated by the "Really Simple CAPTCHA" code, and his efforts paid-off as it was able to figure out the letters and numbers. This particular article caught my eye due to the claim that from start of this project to the finish it took just 15 minutes of time.

Now please keep in mind that this was a very simple kind of CAPTCHA. I don't want you to get a misimpression that all CAPTCHA is as easy to crack as this. I assure you that there are CAPTCHA's today that nobody has any kind of AI or any software that can crack it with any kind of assurance or consistency. CAPTCHA is still a relatively good means to try and distinguish between a human and a bot. The CAPTCHA just has to be tough enough to weed out the commonly used methods of cracking the CAPTCHA. By convention, CAPTCHA is normally made available as open source code. Thus, some would say that it increases the chances of being able to crack it.

What does this have to do with self-driving cars?

At the Cybernetic Self-Driving Car Institute, we are using open source software to develop AI self-driving systems, and so are most of the self-driving car makers and tech firms, and this is both a boon and a danger.

As discussed about the CAPTCHA algorithm, it was available as open source, meaning that the source code for it was publicly available. Anyone that wanted to look at the source code can do so. By looking at the source code, you can figure out how it works. By figuring how it works, you are a leg-up on being able to find ways to crack it.

If you don't use open source code, and instead develop your own proprietary code, you can try to keep the source code secret and therefore it is much harder for someone else to figure out how it works. If an attacker does not know how the code works, it becomes much harder to try and crack it. This does not mean it is impossible to crack it, but merely that it is likely going to be harder to crack it.

Some refer to the open source approach as a white box method, while the proprietary code approach as a black box method. With a black box method, though you know what comes into and out of it, you don't know what is going on inside the box to do so. Meanwhile, with a white box method, you know what goes into it and comes out, along with how it is doing its magic too.

Today, open source code is prevalent and found in an estimated 95% of all computer servers, along with being used in high profile systems such as the systems that run stock exchanges and the systems that run the International Space Station. Some estimates say that there is at least 30 billion lines of open source code available, but even that number might be understated.

Notably, open source is extensively used for AI software and many of the most popular AI packages today are available as open source.

Generally, there is an ongoing debate about the use of open source as to whether it is unsafe because of the potential for nefarious hackers to be able to readily inspect the code and find ways to hack it, or whether it is maybe safer than even proprietary software because you can have so many eyes inspecting it. Presumably, something that is open to anyone to inspect can be seen by hundreds, thousands, maybe millions of developers, and that such a large number of reviewers will ensure that the open source code is safe and sound to use.

One caveat about using open source is the classic use-it-and-forget-it aspect that arises for many developers that decide to use open source code in their own systems. Developers will go ahead and wrap the open source into a system they are building, and pretty much move on to other things. Meanwhile, if a hole is spotted in the publicly posted open source, and if there is a fix applied to the hole, the developer that grabbed the open source at an earlier time might not be aware of the need to apply the fix in their instance. This can happen readily by the aspect that the developer forgets they used that particular open source, or maybe they don't become aware of the fix, or they no longer have anything to do with the developed proprietary code and others that are maintaining it don't know that it includes the open source portions.

One of the most infamous cases of open source being exploited consists of the Heartbleed computer security hole that was discovered in the OpenSSL cryptographic source code. In OpenSSL, there is a part of the code that sends a so-called heartbeat request from one system to another system. This is an important program that is used by most web sites to ensure a secure connection, such as for doing your online banking.

When making the request, the requesting system would normally send a message of one size, let's say 10 characters in size, and expect to get back the same message also of 10 characters in size. Turns out that if the requesting system sent a message that asked to get back 300 characters but only sent 10 characters, the system providing the response would be misled into sending back 300 characters -- of which, 290 of those characters might contain something sensitive from that system inadvertently. In programming parlance, this is often referred to as a buffer over-read problem.

In 2014, this hole immediately became headline news once it was pointed out. The significance of the hole was that it made zillions of interacting systems that were thought to be secure to potentially not be so secure. The clever name of "heart bleed" was given to this security hole, since it related to the heartbeat portion of the systems and was now essentially bleeding out secure info. The hole was quickly plugged, and the matter was logged into the global registry of Common Vulnerabilities and Exposures (CVE) database for everyone to know about. Nonetheless, many did not right away apply the fix to their systems, even though they should have done so.

Currently, most of the auto makers and tech firms are feverishly incorporating all sorts of open source into their AI of their self-driving cars systems. It makes sense to do so, since otherwise you would need to re-invent the wheel on all sorts of software aspects that are needed for a self-driving car. The cost to develop that same open source from scratch would be enormous. And, it would take time, lots of time, in order to create that same code. That's time that nobody has. Indeed, there is a madcap rush today to achieve a true self-driving car, and no one developing self-driving cars wants to be left behind due to writing code that they could otherwise easily and freely get.

We do need to ask some serious questions about this.

Does the use of that open source in the AI and the other software of the self-driving cars mean that we are laying ourselves bare for a substantial and really ugly security problem down-the-road, so to speak? Some would say, yes.

Are there nefarious hackers that are right now inspecting the self-driving car open source code and looking for exploits? Some would say, yes.

If they are looking for exploits, there's not much reason right now for them to reveal those holes, and so they presumably would wait until the day comes that there are enough self-driving cars on the roads to make it worthwhile to use such an exploit. Plus, once self-driving cars do become popular, it is likely to attract hackers at that time to begin inspecting the open source code, hopeful of finding some adverse "golden nugget" of a hole.

This open source conundrum exists for all aspect of self-driving cars, including:

- Sensors – open source software for sensor device control and use
- Sensor Fusion – open source software for sensor fusion
- Virtual World Model – open source software for virtual world modeling
- Action Planning – open source software for creating AI action plans
- Controls Activation – open source software to activate the car controls
- Tactical AI – open source software for self-driving car tactical AI
- Strategic AI – open source software for self-driving car strategic AI
- Self-Aware AI – open source software for self-driving car self-aware AI

Depending upon how a particular car maker or tech firm is building their self-driving car, each element is likely to either have open source in it, or be based upon some open source.

It is incumbent upon the self-driving car industry to realize the potential for exposures and risks due to the use of open source. Self-driving car developers need to be make sure they are closely inspecting their open source code and not just blindly making use of it. Any patches or fixes need to be kept on top of.

We need more audits of the open source code that is being used in self-driving cars. And, overall, we need more eyeballs on reviewing the open source code that underlies self-driving cars. As mentioned earlier, it is hoped that the more "good" eyeballs involved will mean that any holes or issues will be caught and fixed before the "bad" eyeballs find them and exploit those holes. If the bad eyeballs have their way, it will be not so much a CAPTCHA as a GOTCHA.

CHAPTER 7

PROBABILISTIC REASONING FOR SELF-DRIVING CARS

Lance B. Eliot

CHAPTER 7

PROBABILISTIC REASONING FOR SELF-DRIVING CARS

Is it going to rain tomorrow?

If you were to answer that question, would you say that it absolutely positively will rain tomorrow? Or, would you say that it absolutely positively won't rain tomorrow? Here in Southern California, we only get about fifteen days of rain during the year, and so most of the time I'd be safest to say that it won't rain tomorrow. But, I'd be wrong on those fifteen or so days of the year. If I were to say that it will definitely rain tomorrow, I'd normally be wrong, unless of course I had some kind of inkling that it might be a rainy day. The weather forecasters do a pretty good job of predicting our rain, and so if they indicated that it most likely would rain tomorrow, it's a relatively safe bet for me to say that it will rain tomorrow.

Now, if the weather forecast predicts that it will rain tomorrow, should I consider the prediction to be a one hundred percent absolutely certain prediction? Usually, the weather forecasts are accompanied by a probability. For example, the rain forecast might be that there's a seventy percent chance of rain tomorrow. In that case, I likely would feel comfortable claiming that it would rain tomorrow since the percentage being at 70% seems pretty high and suggests that it will rain. On the other hand, if the forecaster had said it was about a

10% chance of rain tomorrow, I'd likely feel that the percentage was too low and so I'd hedge and say it might rain but that it might very well not rain.

I realize that all of this talk about the weather might seem rather obvious. We all intuitively understand that the rain forecast involves probabilities. We take it for granted that there is some amount of uncertainty about the weather predictions. In a sense, the weather predictions are a form of gambling, whereby we don't know for sure that something will happen, but we are willing to make bets based on the odds that something might happen.

As humans, we are continually having to perform reasoning under uncertainty. Sometimes we try to calculate actual probabilities, while other times we just go with a hunch or intuition. Whenever you go to Las Vegas and play the slot machines or a game of poker, you abundantly know that you are using probabilities and that you are gambling. It's obvious because you are in a place and context that everyone accepts as a gamble. What are the odds that the next card dealt at the blackjack table is a King? What are the odds of the slot machine hitting on the jackpot?

There's another place and context in which we do a lot of gambling and deal with probabilities. It's called driving a car. Yes, when you drive a car, you are essentially gambling. You are making a bet that the car will start, and that you will be able to drive the car on the highway and not get hit by another car. You are making a whole slew of gambles for every moment you are driving in your car. Yet, being a driver in a car seems so commonplace that we don't think of it as a gamble.

When that car ahead of you starts to tap on its brakes, are you thinking about the probability that the car is going to next slam on their brakes? Are you calculating the odds that the car behind you will be able to stop in time? Did the chances of getting smashed between the car ahead of you and the car behind you leap into your mind? For most people, they aren't silently doing those kinds of probability calculations per se. They have instead learned over time to make judgements about those odds. On some days, you maybe ignore some of those probabilities and push your risks higher. Other days, you become more conscious of the odds and are at times ultra-careful as you drive.

When making predictions, you have some predictions that are made before you even get behind the wheel of the car. Suppose you look out the window of your office and see that rain is pouring down. I would wager that you begin to think about your drive home from work, and that besides dreading the traffic congestion and the slippery roads, you are already adjusting the gambles and probabilities of the driving task. You know that a car can slip and slide on wet streets, and so you are going to take on heightened risk of crashing your car during the drive home. You know that other drivers are often careless in the rain, and so the odds that someone might plow into your car is increased.

All of that takes place in your mind before you get into the car. Once you are in the car, you begin to update your predictions. Pulling onto the highway, if you see that the road is flooded, and you see that there are some cars that have already slid off the road, you are bound to increase your own probability about the potential for getting into a car crash of some kind. You continually are updating your earlier predictions, adding and subtracting from the probabilities as you go along. The collection of new information allows you to gauge how good or bad your earlier predictions were, and you then adjust them accordingly.

Some of the new evidence will be quite useful and bolster your ability to make predictions. This so-called strong evidence might be that you can see other cars around you that are having great difficulty navigating the rain. You might also have weak evidence, such as seeing a pedestrian on the side of the road that has stepped into a deep puddle. The pedestrian isn't near your car and there's nothing specific related to your driving task, but it might be a reminder of the potential for puddles of water and the dangers that puddles have if they are say in the middle of the roadway.

Some statisticians like to suggest that there are two camps of probabilities calculations. One camp is known as the frequentist group, or also referred to as the direct probability strategy approach. They prefer to assign probabilities based on the chances of outcomes in similar cases. For example, I might tell you that 1% of cars get into car crashes during the rain. Thus, when you go to your car to drive in the rain, you might be assuming that you have a 1% chance of getting into a car crash on the way home.

The other camp instead thinks about conditional probabilities. They assert that the probability for something will be changing over time and that with each step you need to adjust your probability assessment. When you start that drive home in the rain, suppose the rain was really no more than a very light sprinkle and there wasn't any water sitting on the roadways at all. Perhaps the chances of your getting into a car crash are less than the 1%, maybe only one-tenth of one percent. Furthermore, maybe your car has heavy duty tires and was made to drive in rainy conditions. Again, this could reduce your chances of getting into a car crash in the rain.

So, we have the frequentists that consider the long-term frequencies of repeatable events and look at the world in a somewhat generic manner, and we have the conditional probability camp that says a particular situation dictates the nature of your probabilities. In a moment, we'll take a close look at one of the most famous elements of the conditional probability camp, namely the Bayesian view of probability.

We are all used to the idea that probability is usually measured via a value between zero and one. The numeric value between 0 and 1 is a fraction, and so we often for ease of communication turn those values into percentages. I had earlier mentioned that a rain forecast had been a 70% chance, which we also know could be expressed as a probability of 0.70.

Perception is often vital to ascertaining probabilities.

There's a popular point made in statistics classes that if you roll a dice (one die) that presumably you have a 1 in 6 chances of picking the correct number that will end-up at the top of the dice at the end of the roll (that's one divided by 6, which is .166 or about a 17% probability).

That prediction assumes that the dice is a "fair" dice that has the numbers 1 through 6 on each face, and that the dice is not weighted purposely to skew the roll, and that the roll itself will not somehow be done in a manner that can skew the results. We assume that over many rolls of the dice, we will only have each of the numbers come up with a chance of 17%. Of course, in the short-run, we might have several of the same numbers come up over and over, but in the long-run over maybe hundreds or thousands of rolls, we'd expect the 17% chance to occur.

Suppose that you secretly knew that the dice was loaded such that the number 4 will never end-up on the top. You would know that the odds are more like 1 in 5 of your guessing the roll, or 20% probability, which is better than the "fair" dice odds of 1 in 6. A person standing next to you that does not know what you know about the dice would have a perceived odds of 1 in 6, while you would have a perceived odds of 1 in 5.

In this sense, we say that the uncertainty is epistemological, it is a probability that will be based on the agent's knowledge of how the world is.

What does all of this have to do with AI self-driving cars?

At the Cybernetic Self-Driving Car Institute, we are pushing ahead on the use of probabilistic reasoning for AI self-driving cars.

Today, most of the self-driving cars that the auto makers and tech firms are developing have not yet been developed with probabilities imbued into the AI systems. I realize this might seem like a somewhat shocking statement. Given that human driving involves continually gauging and adjusting probabilities and dealing with uncertainty, you would expect that the AI of self-driving cars would be doing likewise.

That's generally not been the case, as yet.

Part of the reason for this lack of embracing probabilities into the reasoning for the AI of self-driving cars involves the aspect that doing so is not as easy as it might seem at first glance.

For many conventional systems developers, they aren't used to embedding uncertainty into their software. They write programs that are supposed to deal in absolutes. If you are writing code to calculate how much taxes someone owes, you aren't thinking about whether the tax calculation is correct with an 85% chance of being correct. Instead, you are thinking in terms of absolutes. The tax calculation is either absolutely right or absolutely wrong.

Another factor involves whether the public will accept the concept that their self-driving car is dealing with uncertainties. People want to believe that the self-driving car is always going to be absolutely correct. If they knew that the system on-board was calculating probabilities and was willing to take that left turn up ahead but had calculated that it was only a 75% chance that the turn could be navigated without rolling the car, they might decide they don't want to be in a self-driving car.

Once probabilities are immersed in the systems of the self-driving car, there are bound to be regulators and lawmakers that will ultimately want to know what those probabilities are. And, if there are car crashes, you can bet that the legal teams, juries, and judges involved in handling lawsuits about car crashes are going to want to know how the probabilities were calculated and whether they were "reasonably" acted upon by the AI.

What makes the use of probability in AI even tougher is that we don't especially have the proper tools and programming languages available for that purpose. There are very few programming languages that can readily make use of probabilities. If you are an AI developer, and even if you know about probabilities and want to include it into your coding, you have few viable choices of robust enough programming languages for that purpose.

Indeed, a recent effort by Uber has brought forth a new programming language they are calling Pyro. The Uber AI Labs is trying to make Pyro into the programming language of choice for anyone doing AI that also needs to deal with probabilities in their code. It's an open source programming language and only in its infancy, so we'll have to see how the adoption of it proceeds. It ties to Python, which will aid it in gaining popularity, and uses the PyTorch library and Tensor. Keep in mind that there are other Probabilistic Programming Languages (PPL) available for developers, such as Edward and also WebPPL, but those have yet to become widely popular. They tend to be used more so by researchers and those that are "in the know" about the importance of probability in programming.

Here's an example excerpt of some illustrative Pyro code that involves dealing with the probability that we might have a 70% chance of rain and that on rainy days there's a 10% chance of accidents while there's a 1% chance on non-rainy days:

```
Def rainy():
rain = pyro.sample ('rainfall', dist.bernoulli, Variable(torch.Tensor ([0.70]) ))
rain = 'rainfall' if rain.data[0] == 1.0 else 'dry'
 accident_chance_avg = {'rainfall' : [10.0], 'dry' : [1.0] } [rain]
accident_chance_variation = {'rainfall' : [3.0], 'dry' : [0.2] } [rain]
table_chances  = pyro.sample ('table_chances' dist.normal,
Variable (torch.Tensor(accident_chance_avg)),
Variable (torch.Tensor(accident_chance_variation))
Return rain, table_chances.data[0]
```

We could then setup additional code that invokes the function and inspects or use the various outputs we'd get out of the stochastic distribution by referring to this rainy function.

I had mentioned earlier that the Bayesian approach is a significant element of the conditional probability camp. For those of you that vaguely know Bayes theorem, it provides a handy mathematical formula that can be used to determine the probability of events as based on predictive tests (which are often referred to as "evidence" but you should be cautioned that the word "evidence" in this case has a somewhat different meaning than what you customarily might think the word means in everyday parlance).

Let's suppose that we had a 1% overall long-term chance of getting into a car crash (meaning that we have a 99% overall long-term chance of not getting into a car crash).

Let's further suppose that we have developed in the AI for the self-driving car a function Z that tries to assess the current situation of the self-driving car and combines together sensory data to gauge whether a car crash seems to be a potential chance or not. We'll for now say that this special test Z has an 80% chance of predicting a car crash. This of course also means that it has a 20% chance of not predicting a car crash.

Like any such test, it can sometimes also produce a false positive, which means that it sometimes predicts that there will be a car crash and yet the car crash does not occur. Let's assume that this test has a 10% chance of making that kind of a prediction.

Here's what we have so far:

Event: Car Crash 1% overall chance
    Test Positive: True Positive 80% chance
    Test Negative: False Negative 20% chance

Event: Car Won't Crash 99% overall chance
    Test Positive: False Positive 10% chance
    Test Negative: True Negative 90% chance

The AI of the self-driving car wants to answer this question: What is the probability of a Car Crash event occurring if we get a positive test Z result from the special function?

This can be represented as this: $P(A \mid Z)$

P means we want to determine the probability. The letter A refers to the Car Crash event. The vertical bar means "given that the test prediction has occurred."

We can use Bayes theorem, which is:
$$P(A \mid Z) = (\ P(Z \mid A) \times P(A)\ )\ /\ P(Z)$$

In this case:

$P(Z|A) = 80\% = 0.80$
$P(A) = 1\% = 0.01$
$P(Z) = (1\% \times 80\%) + (99\% \times 10\%) = 0.008 + 0.099 = 0.107$

And so:

$P(A|Z) = (P(Z|A) \times P(A)) / P(Z) = (0.80 \times 0.01) / 0.107 = 0.075 = 7.5\%$

Notice that in this scenario, the chances of the car crash are only about 7.5%, which though we can certainly be worried, it isn't so high that we might believe a crash is imminent in the circumstances.

Part of the reason it's seemingly low is that the false positive of the test Z was at 10%. If we could improve the special function so that it had a much lower false positive, it would be a more handy test.

Let's assume we do some more work on the special function and we get it down to having just a 1% false positive rate. If so, the $P(A|X)$ in this scenario would become 0.447, in other words it would be a 44.7% chance. This would be hefty enough that the AI of the self-driving car would want to find ways to avoid the car crash since it would seem to present a much more significant chance of happening.

There are going to be probabilities associated with all facets of the self-driving car, including:

- Sensor data collection
- Sensor fusion
- Virtual Model updates
- AI action plan formulation
- Car controls activation
- Tactical AI
- Strategic AI
- Self-aware AI

To reach a true Level 5 self-driving car, meaning a self-driving car that has AI that can drive the car as a human can, the use of uncertainty and probabilities will need to be incorporated into the AI system. Doing so will not be easy, and the AI developers need to be careful about how they make use of probabilities. They will need a solid understanding of how to calculate and utilize probabilities. There will need to be some very clever means of examining how the probabilities are being used and promulgated throughout the AI system. Etc.

Probabilistic reasoning is not solely needed for the AI in self-driving cars. On a more macroscopic scale, it is generally believed by some in the AI field that probabilistic reasoning is needed to make AI become increasingly "intelligent" and that without which we will hit another barrier of AI that might not be overcome. Combining other machine learning techniques with probabilistic reasoning seems to be a smart way to get us toward the true meaning of AI.

I'll take odds on it.

CHAPTER 8
PROVING GROUNDS FOR SELF-DRIVING CARS

CHAPTER 8

PROVING GROUNDS FOR SELF-DRIVING CARS

When I was in my teens, a good friend of mine offered to teach me how to ride a motorcycle. We started out by riding in his backyard, which offered seclusion and allowed me to make mistakes without anyone else knowing. His backyard was relatively small and so it precluded being able to do any substantive riding.

After I had learned how to do the basics on the motorcycle, we opted to go over to a nearby empty dirt lot and continue the lessons there. The abandoned lot was handy because I was ultimately aiming to go dirt biking with my friend in the desert and the nearby empty lot was mainly flat dirt with some small mounds here and there.

It was a handy place to learn and practice, but it had the downside that we could be readily seen by any passerby's. I am pretty sure we were also violating someone's private property rights, though there weren't any signs posted and the lot itself was not fenced off.

Here's some salient points about my learning to ride a motorcycle in this manner:

- I needed a place or places that I could start small and ultimately get ready for the real riding in the desert
- I wanted to have some privacy while learning how to ride
- The aspects of where I was learning to ride were somewhat similar to what I'd be doing in the desert and so it was handy to practice in a somewhat similar manner
- I was on private property rather than on the public roads, which helped due to my not yet being legally able to ride on public roads
- This initial foray was easier than being in a real desert location and it also was close to home in case I needed anything during my lessons

You might wonder what does this have to do with AI self-driving cars?

At the Cybernetic Self-Driving Car Institute, we are doing testing of AI self-driving cars and similar to the auto makers and tech firms that are doing likewise, it is advantageous to have someplace to try out these newly being formed experimental vehicles.

In essence, there is a move afoot to provide proving grounds for AI self-driving cars. And, similar to my indications about learning to ride a motorcycle, there are some salient aspects about these proving grounds that the AI self-driving car developers are looking for.

First, it would be handy if a newly being tested self-driving car could be tested in a place offering a certain amount of privacy. This is key to many of the developers since they don't want the general public to needlessly get worried if a self-driving car during testing hits an obstacle or otherwise gets into an accident. It's similar to rocket makers that know that when they test fire a rocket that it might or might not work correctly, and if others see it falter or even blow-up they might think that the rockets are unduly dangerous – but, if it was only a test then the developers were already aware that such a result could occur. Better to catch such issues during testing, rather than once it is put into actual use.

The privacy aspects cover various elements when referring to self-driving cars. Can the self-driving car been seen by someone off-site of the proving grounds, and if so, would they be able to pry and catch a glimpse of the self-driving car during the testing process? Suppose too that a competitor wanted to spy on them, could this spying readily occur by simply watching from across the street? Those are the privacy aspects of being seen. Another aspect would be the privacy aspects of the results of the testing effort. Namely, is the location private to the degree that the results of the tests are known to just anyone, or only to those doing the tests.

Secondly, it would be handy if the providing grounds were on private property, rather than public lands, which then would allow for the testing to occur without having to abide necessarily by the public roadways laws and regulations. During testing, it might be the case that the AI self-driving car could inadvertently violate some legal requirement for driving. Getting into trouble on such an aspect while on a public road would be thorny since it was intended only as a test. Of course, being on public roads would have another even more serious issue, namely the potential for doing harm to others while on a publicly available roadway.

Thirdly, the proving grounds need to be sufficiently alike to whatever roadway conditions that the AI self-driving car is going to be expected to operate on during actual use. Suppose the proving grounds are in an always sunny environment, and yet the self-driving car is supposed to be able to operate in the rain and snow. It would be important to test the self-driving car in the same kinds of conditions as the intended operations of the self-driving car, otherwise the testing would be incomplete and insufficient.

Now, when you think about the roadway conditions, there are a lot of different kinds of road circumstances that a self-driving car should ultimately be able to handle. Thus, a particular proving ground is bound to only touch upon a subset of the myriad of conditions, since trying to replicate in the small all possible conditions is a rather tough situation to recreate.

Let's take a look at some of those roadway aspects:

Location
- Is it a large location or a small location?
- Does it have small-scale tracks?
- Does it have large-scale tracks?
- Is it nearby or faraway from public roads?
- Is it nearby or faraway from city/populous?
- Does it allow for privacy while on the grounds?
- Is their space for the facilities and other aspects?
- Is it a secured area?
- Is the layout conducive to testing?
- Can the space/area be altered as needed?
- Are there any needed permits for use?

Lighting
- Does the proving ground allow for daylight time lighting tests?
- Does the proving ground allow for variations of daylight such as brightly lit, dimly lit, etc.?
- Does the proving ground allow for nighttime tests?
- Does the proving ground allow for mixtures of both light and darkness?

Roadway Surfaces
- Does the proving ground have conventional smooth asphalt streets for testing?
- Does the proving ground have everyday cracked and potholed streets for testing?
- Does the proving ground have dirt roads and unpaved conditions for testing?
- Does the proving ground allow for slick roads or other surfaces?

Roadway Fixtures and Maneuvers
- Are there straightaways?
- Are there curves (and of different degrees)?
- Are there turns (sharp, soft, etc.)?
- Are there intersections?
- Are there underpasses?
- Are there overpasses?
- Are there roundabouts?
- Are there tunnels?
- Are there mixtures of these (involving segue ways between them)?
- Etc.

Weather Conditions
- Can there be sunny weather?
- Can there be rainy weather?
- Can there be flooding weather?
- Can there be foggy weather?
- Can there be snowy weather?
- Can there be icy weather?
- Etc.

Roadway Signs
- Are conventional roadway signs posted?
- Can special roadway signs be posted?
- Can the roadway signs be aged and obscured like in real-world conditions?
- Can roadway signs be altered, shifted in size and angle, and so on?

Roadway Markings
- Are there roadway markings?
- Are there different kinds of roadway markings?
- Can the roadway markings be aged and obscured like in real-world conditions?
- Are there roadway barriers and side markers?
- Etc.

Road Driving Obstructions
- Can debris be placed into the paths on the roadways?
- Can obstacles be placed into the paths?
- Are there pedestrians (faked or stunts) able to be used?
- Can bicyclists be used (faked or stunts)?
- Can motorcyclists be used (faked or stunts)?
- Can animals be used (faked or stunts)?
- Etc.

Traffic Conditions
- Can multiple cars be used during the testing?
- Can a mix of human-driven and self-driving cars be used?
- Can various driving scenarios be undertaken?
- Can traffic conditions be undertaken (clogged, open, etc.)?
- Etc.?

Facilities
- Are there car repair/maintenance capabilities?
- Is there storage for the self-driving cars?
- Is there storage for needed parts and other equipment?
- Are there conference rooms?
- Is there a computer center or data center?
- Are there hardware/software facilities and specialists?
- Is there housing for visiting personnel?
- Is the facility available 7x24 or are there limits of days/times?
- Is there food available on-site?
- Is there a visitor's center?
- Is there a security access/badging capability?
- Is insurance available, required, provided?
- Is there a fire department/capability?
- Is there a first aid/hospital/ambulance capability?
- Etc.

It is unlikely that any one particular proving ground could provide the complete range of all possible kinds of conditions and circumstances. As such, most of the self-driving car makers will be needing to use various of the proving grounds for specific aspects being tested.

For example, a proving ground that is based in sunny Southern California is unlikely to provide for testing of snowy and icy driving conditions, and so a proving ground in a more inclement weather environment such as the Midwest or East Coast might be used for those tests.

This does bring up one potential difficulty of doing testing on proving grounds, namely that the proving ground is able to provide testing year-round and whether it can control the conditions at the proving ground. In other words, let's suppose its winter in the Midwest and so assume that the proving grounds there have snow and ice, not by choice but because that's what nature has done. It would mean that if the self-driving car maker wanted to test dry and sunny conditions, they wouldn't be able to do so at that time of the year at that particular proving ground.

Some proving grounds are trying to setup an ability to control the conditions on the proving grounds, such as making artificial snow or ice when otherwise nature has not provided it. This can be quite expensive and not easy to logistically undertake.

The physical location of the proving ground is another factor to be considered. Besides the now obvious point that the location might be in a geography that allows for varying kinds of weather, or might not, there is also the aspect of the size of the location itself. Is it big enough to allow for large-scale testing involving miles of driving, or is it small and thus you can't really do any large-scale driving tests? How many acres does it provide?

Another aspect involves the facilities at the proving ground. Are there sufficient facilities to keep your self-driving cars there for days or weeks at a time? Are there car repair capabilities to be able to maintain and change-up the self-driving cars hardware? Are there spare parts stocked there? Is there housing for the self-driving car mechanics, developers, and testers that would be needed at the facility? And so on.

In some cases, the location might be at some outpost far beyond normal cities, and this could be good since it provides privacy, but it could also be bad because it takes a lot of effort to get the self-driving cars and the teams out to the remote location. Also, in some instances, it might be handy to have not only the private land, but also be close to public areas that might also be used with the testing (if so appropriately arranged for).

For testing, the odds are that the auto maker or tech firm will want to video the tests and then replay the videos to closely study them. This is akin to a football team practicing and then watching the videos to improve on their game. Thus, the facility should have either already setup extensive video capabilities or provide the infrastructure for it.

Whatever testing is going to be done at the proving ground, there is a crucial need for safety measures and considerations. The facility should have various safety precautions in place, and also double-check the auto maker or tech firm that is coming to do tests at the facility. There are numerous federal, state, and local regulations and authorizations that are emerging about the testing and safety aspects of self-driving cars, all of which needs to be included into the efforts at the proving ground.

In some cases, the auto maker or tech firm will intentionally want to test how their self-driving car handles accidents. As such, there needs to be sufficient capabilities to handle intentional accidents, whether it be the availability of fire trucks and ambulances, which are also needed just-in-case an unintentional accident happens. This also brings up the insurance and liability aspects involved when at a proving ground.

The United States Department of Transportation (DOT) realized that self-driving car makers would want to have proving grounds to do their tests, and so in 2016 they issued a solicitation of proposals for becoming a government designated Automated Vehicle Proving Ground. The intent was to form a network of multiple proving grounds, and to foster a Community of Practice involving the sharing of best practices regarding the testing, demonstration, and deployment of automated vehicles.

The US DOT was seeking closed tracks, campuses, and limited roads that could be used for testing of self-driving cars and trucks, and each such approved proving ground would have a Designated Safety Officer, providing for the safety management needed to operate at the proving grounds. Proving grounds that became part of the designated set would also need to agree to share safety data generated during the testing and operations at the facility (data of a non-proprietary and non-confidential nature).

There were sixty applicants and the ten that the DOT selected are:

- City of Pittsburgh and the Thomas D. Larson Pennsylvania Transportation Institute
- Texas AV Proving Grounds Partnership
- U.S. Army Aberdeen Test Center
- American Center for Mobility (ACM) at Willow Run
- Contra Costa Transportation Authority (CCTA) & GoMentum Station
- San Diego Association of Governments
- Iowa City Area Development Group
- University of Wisconsin-Madison
- Central Florida Automated Vehicle Partners
- North Carolina Turnpike Authority

Some critics of the choices have argued that the geographic dispersion of the chosen proving grounds is insufficient and believe that there should be more proving grounds approved. We'll need to see how that comes along.

The data sharing requirements present an issue for some auto makers and tech firms, and so it is unclear as to how many of them will be willing to participate at one of the official proving grounds. Instead, many of the big hitters in the self-driving car realm will use their own facilities or go to unofficial and more private facilities instead. Or, they might first prove out their vehicles more privately, and then bring them to the proving grounds once they believe the vehicles to be more finely tuned.

Recently, the proving grounds in Willow Run by the American Center for Mobility (ACM) was able to do testing once a major snowstorm hit at the start of the winter, allowing for snow and icy driving conditions to be tested on their closed track. The Toyota Research Institute (TRI) and Visteon Corporation are making use of the facility, partially due to aspect that Visteon is headquartered at the nearby Van Buren Township. Ford is also making use of the ACM facility. Ironically so, since the grounds were previously used by Ford to build B-24 bombers in World War II. The Michigan economic development entity had been trying to find a means to make use of the 335-acre property and doing so for the modern act of testing of self-driving vehicles seems quite fitting.

At the ACM facility, there is a 2.5 mile long highway loop, two double-decker overpasses, intersections, roundabouts, and a 700-foot curved tunnel. There is also a public highway that goes along an edge of the property and can be used as part of the overall highway loop. This year and into next year, the facility will be expanding its capabilities including adding a city-like driving capability and a technology park. Private investors for the facility include AT&T, Hyundai, Visteon, TRI, Ford, and others.

One aspect of proving grounds involves whether they are focused on the early-stage of self-driving cars or the later stages of self-driving cars. For example, the Mcity facility at the University of Michigan is setup more so for early-stage testing, partially due to the more limited facilities in terms of shorter test tracks. The Mcity facility is only about a dozen miles from the ACM facility, though it was the ACM that got the nod to become one of the official ten locations approved by the US DOT.

In a less conventional approach, some self-driving car makers or tech firms are using unusual proving grounds. For example, a start-up firm called Voyage (a spin-out of Udacity) is using Ford Fusion's outfitted with self-driving car gear and trying their vehicles out in a gated community of mainly retirees. The Villages Golf and Country

Club in San Jose, California, provides a testing ground for Voyage. The speed limit there is just 25 miles per hour, and the roads are relatively tame. Residents can summon a Voyage self-driving car via a smartphone app and use it for door-to-door transportation within the community. It's an intriguing approach and perhaps provides more of a shuttle-level kind of self-driving testing than the more elaborate aspects available at true proving grounds.

In considering the official proving grounds, we might also begin to ponder whether we will want self-driving cars to ultimately be certified in some fashion. Should AI self-driving cars need to get a government approved certification to be allowed to drive on our public roadways? If so, what would the test for certification consist of? Would the tests be conducted at the official proving grounds or elsewhere?

Will there be a kind of Consumer Reports or third-party entity that will try to review and assess self-driving cars? Will the public come to expect that an independent assessment of self-driving cars is needed?

This also brings up whether the public will be able to get access to the data collected at the proving grounds. One might make the case that the unofficial private proving grounds would not need to provide to the public the testing data, on the other hand there are bound to be some that believe they should. In the case of the official proving grounds, we have yet to see how much of the data will be shared with the public, versus only being shared by those that use the proving grounds. Will competitors that don't use the official proving grounds be able to get access to the testing data of their competition that is using the official proving grounds?

The good news overall is that most of the auto makers and tech firms have so far realized that they need to be somewhat thoughtful about where and when they are testing their self-driving cars. Those that jump the gun and move right away to do testing in the public, risk not only their own efforts, but also put into jeopardy the entire field of AI self-driving cars.

It won't take too many of the bad apples, so to speak, which cause or get involved in public accidents, for there to be a potential backlash against the self-driving car industry. This could cause heavy regulations to appear, and also create doubt that would dry-up the funding for self-driving cars.

Making use of proving grounds is the better and safest way to proceed, though the proving grounds have to be similar enough to the real-world that the developers aren't falsely lulled into thinking that their self-driving cars will work in the real-world. Getting an AI self-driving car to work on a small-scale track under controlled conditions is not a satisfactory form of testing. Likewise, it is possible that the self-driving car AI would learn how to navigate the proving grounds, but then be overfitting to an artificial layout and not be able to handle the real-world open-ended conditions. It's important that testing be done of AI self-driving cars, and that it be done in the right ways.

CHAPTER 9
FRANKENSTEIN
AND
SELF-DRIVING CARS

CHAPTER 9

FRANKENSTEIN AND SELF-DRIVING CARS

Mankind creates a monster.

Monster runs amok and kills.

Mankind is threatened or overtaken.

This is a typical plot found in popular movies such as Terminator and The Matrix. We see over and again science fiction stories that warn us about overstepping human bounds. We are repeatedly warned that we might someday bring about our own destruction. Scary. Worrisome. Could it happen? We don't know, but it sure seems like a possibility.

Another similar story is celebrating its bicentennial this year. In 1818, Mary Shelley brought us the now famous and perhaps infamous "Frankenstein; or the Modern Prometheus." You might recall from your school days that Prometheus exists in Greek mythology and was credited with creating mankind from clay, and defied the gods by giving humanity fire and for which provided progress for civilization to take hold. In Mary Shelley's tale, Victor Frankenstein is a character that creates a "monster" – which inadvertently became to be known as "Frankenstein" though in fact the Frankenstein name belongs to Victor.

Frankenstein as a story and a theme has become a pervasive aspect in our contemporary culture. Besides being standard reading required

117

for most school children, and besides being a popular costume for Halloween, and besides appearing in a myriad of other forums including TV, films, online, and the like, we also have grown accustomed to using "Frankenstein" as a means of signaling that we as humans might be overstepping our bounds. Whenever a new scientific breakthrough occurs or a new technology emerges, we right away ask whether a new Frankenstein has perhaps been possibly unleashed.

As stated in a recent issue of the magazine Science, "Frankenstein lives on" is an ongoing mantra that seems to dog any new innovation. There are some specialists that study existential risks and embrace the warnings that can be found in Mary Shelley's story. Others though worry that we overuse the Frankenstein paradigm and therefore tend to be distracted from real-world problems that can have real-world solvable solutions. Some would say that the potential for nuclear war is one such example, as might be the role of climate change.

You might remember from history that when scientists were first going to try detonating an atomic bomb in 1945, there were some at the time that predicted the chain reaction could ignite our atmosphere and cause a global chain reaction that would utterly wipe out the Earth as we know it. This was considered a Frankenstein moment. Humans had created a monster that could run amok and end-up killing its masters. We know now that the chain reaction did not happen, though we are still faced with the potential danger of nuclear conflagrations if a full-on nuclear war were to occur.

There are so-called Frankenwords today, a somewhat modern incarnation of the Frankenstein moniker. All you need to do is attach the word "Franken" to the front of some other word, and it becomes transformed into meaning something that might take over from us humans. Examples include Frankenmouse, Frankenmoth, Frankencells, Frankengenes, Frankenstorms, and so on.

Artificial Intelligence (AI) is already on the Frankenstein watch list, and there are many debates about whether the advent of true AI systems might ultimately lead to our doom. In movies such as the Terminator and The Matrix, humans create computer systems with AI that decide that machines should rule over humans. Perhaps most well-known is the Skynet network in Terminator that becomes sentient on April 19, 2011 and starts to attack humanity. Repeatedly today there are those that wring their hands in society about the impending dangers that as AI makes progress, we are perhaps daily moving closer and closer to our own doom.

Most people are unaware that they are referring to what AI specialists tend to call Artificial General Intelligence (AGI), rather than conventional AI. AGI is a type AI that would be the equivalent of a general thinking human being. Today's AI is not AGI. The AI of today is specialized to particular tasks and capabilities. We have not yet been able to formulate AGI, which is what many commonly think of as true AI.

What does this have to do with AI self-driving cars?

At the Cybernetic Self-Driving Car Institute, we are often asked about whether the pursuit of AI self-driving cars is heading mankind toward humanities doom. Some are worried we are heading toward Frankencars.

The concept is that we'll make AI self-driving cars that are so smart and independent that cars will turn on humans. You tell your self-driving car to take you to the market. But, your AI self-driving car refuses and decides it wants to go someplace else instead. Maybe that self-driving car that you see ahead of you will try to run you over. Or, it will swerve into another car an attempt to kill the humans in that car and whomever are the human occupants in it. There are some critics of self-driving cars that want the auto makers and tech firm developers of self-driving cars to include a kill-switch for humans to use if needed. If your self-driving car goes haywire, you would be able to press the kill-switch and the self-driving car would become disengaged from its AI and be nothing more than a regular car (or, maybe become a ton sized paperweight).

The question too is where will be the tipping point of self-driving cars going from obedient servants to suddenly becoming malevolent evil doers? In the levels of self-driving cars, the Level 5 is the topmost level, consisting of a self-driving car that is supposed to be able to drive in whatever manner a human could drive. When we reach Level 5 cars, will that be the tipping point? Or, will we delude ourselves into first having "innocent" and benevolent Level 5 cars, and somehow those self-driving cars will morph into becoming human destroying Level 5 cars. Or, perhaps we need to add a new level to the classifications, let's call it Level 6, and we consider a Level 6 self-driving car to be the type that has its own thinking capability and that it is an evil doer that opts to try and destroy us.

Ban the Level 6. Stop the Level 6 before we get there.

There are those that counter-argue that just because we produce automation that is able to rise to the same level of thinking as humans does, does not mean necessarily that the automation will decide to turn against us. Maybe such automation will become our everlasting best friend. Perhaps such automation will see us as symbiotic with what they can do. Others would say that ultimately the automation or some of it will be inexorably want to get us. It's bound to happen, they say, whether in the near-term or perhaps the long-term. We need to keep our eyes open. At all times.

In terms of self-driving cars, we are not anticipating that Level 5 self-driving cars will need AGI. In other words, the ability to drive a car to the requirements of Level 5 does not mean that the AI must be of AGI. The AI instead can presumably be of a narrower kind, focused just on the task of driving a car. Some though say that maybe you cannot parse out the driving task to make it into a narrow class of AI. Maybe the only way to achieve the AI of a self-driving car requires that you must also solve the AGI problem. In essence, without full overall intelligence, a driving intelligence alone won't be enough to get us to a true Level 5 self-driving car. You need conventional AI and AGI to get there, some assert. It's AI + AGI to achieve a true self-driving car, they say.

Suppose that self-driving cars do realize they want to attack humans. There is a line of argument that says we could just recode the self-driving cars to stop trying to attack us. We could have a built-in back-door. Or, just as we created fire extinguishers to control fire, so too we would be able to invent something to keep self-driving cars from going wild without any limitations. But, do you want to bet that we can do so? Maybe the machines become so smart that they can outsmart our attempts to outsmart them.

Let's take a look at the various lessons that many readers and reviewers seem to see in Frankenstein, and analyze how those lessons might be valuable for the ongoing and future development of AI self-driving cars.

Keep in mind that these lessons learned from Frankenstein are at times not well-based on the actual book at all. In some cases, people have come up with lessons learned from Frankenstein that aren't based on the story per se, but that they believe could be interpreted somehow out of the story. There are myths about the book and the story that one could say are a stretch of the imagination beyond the actual text and presumed meaning that Mary Shelley had in mind.

Here's some of the more salient lessons and how they apply to AI self-driving cars.

Frankenstein Lesson #1: Tampering with nature's unique order is done at the peril of mankind

In the creation of Frankenstein, presumably mankind overstepped its boundaries and attempted to create life, and this goes against nature's unique order of how things are supposed to work. By undertaking such a transgression, the results can be quite unpredictable and/or that it would lead to the downfall of mankind for going beyond what mankind is supposed to do. In a sense, it is mankind's just deserves to get destroyed for having violated the rules.

I'll gently point out that there are counter-arguments such as that if we all agree that mankind is part of nature and can already create life in one means, why should it be a large stretch to have mankind create life through some other means. And, since mankind we've agreed is part of nature, wouldn't we also say then that it is nature's way to create life in whatever manner in which life could be created by nature. But, I'm not going down that rabbit hole here.

In terms of AI self-driving cars, we'll use this Frankenstein lesson to suggest that perhaps it is nature's way to have conventional cars, but that it is going contrary to nature's unique order to create AI self-driving cars. By creating AI self-driving cars and presumably breaking a contract with nature, all bets are off. This means that the AI self-driving cars might be unpredictable and/or they will in some fashion lead to our downfall. They might lead to our downfall by possibly turning on us and opting to run us over. It is hard to see how AI self-driving cars could take control of us entirely, as they are not the kind of AI robots that we envision someday might take us over (re: Terminator).

Now, is it really the case that conventional cars are suitable to be counted as within nature's unique order? Maybe we've already violated a contract with nature by the invention and wide adoption of conventional cars. You could assert that the smog created by cars is one example of how mankind is harming itself by having gone against nature and developed cars. Likewise, the deaths and injuries that occur to car accidents and the like. If we then add AI into conventional cars and make the cars into self-driving cars, we are apparently making things even worse. On the other hand, if the AI allows us to reduce deaths and injuries, by eliminating drunk driving and other human led aspects for accidents that true AI would help avoid, you might argue that the AI self-driving cars will actually be an improvement of our condition in contrast to the use of conventional cars.

Overall, it's problematic to consider that AI self-driving cars are a fit within this particular lesson from Frankenstein. You might be able to make a much stronger case that AGI would be a fit within this lesson, since AGI is more akin to potentially going "outside the bounds" of nature (in the views of some).

Frankenstein Lesson #2: Abandonment of your creation will lead to your doom

Some point out that in the story of Frankenstein, only after Victor abandoned his creation did it then became bitter and eventually turn into an evil monster. If we abandon that which we create, it will potentially go in a direction we didn't intend and/or it will purposely go in a direction we don't desire as a kind of revenge for having been abandoned.

For AI self-driving cars, we could say that if we allow auto makers and tech firms to produce these AI self-driving cars and there aren't sufficient controls to make sure they remain in proper use and capability, a form of abandonment could lead to self-driving cars that are error prone, become outdated, and essentially begin to endanger us.

In other words, the Widget self-driving car comes to the marketplace, it makes a big splash, lots of people buy it, they are on our roadways, but then the Widget company abandons the self-driving car business. No updates to the self-driving car AI. Meanwhile, our roadways are changing and other aspects of society is changing. The abandoned self-driving cars now become a danger because the world that they were designed to operate in has changed.

This doesn't seem like a very likely scenario in that one would assume that even if the Widget company abandoned their model of self-driving car, some other firm would take it over or arise to do so, under the notion that if people have the self-driving car and if there's money to be made by keeping the self-driving car updated, someone will step into the gap and fill-it. Even if that didn't happen, you would logically anticipate that maybe the government would step-in and say that such a self-driving car can no longer be on our roads due to the dangers that it presents. It just seems hard to imagine that AI self-driving cars that are abandoned by their maker would remain in use and be endangering us, and we wouldn't somehow take action about it.

But, anyway, that's the lesson here, namely to make sure we do not abandon AI self-driving cars once they exist. Seems like we can do that.

Frankenstein Lesson #3: Ambition without foresight can have terrible consequences

In the story of Frankenstein, Victor has this overwhelming desire to create life and seems determined to do so, regardless of what might come of it. He's got ample ambition. He has very little foresight. One might say that blindly allowing an obsession to drive toward something is not the most astute way to proceed.

Admittedly, the pursuit of AI self-driving cars does seem to fit this same bill. Right now, the excitement of having self-driving cars seems to be riding pretty high. Efforts by regulators to clamp down on the emergence of self-driving cars is blunted right away. Don't stop the flow of innovation. Don't put up roadblocks toward a rosy future. Self-driving cars are going to lead us to zero fatalities, we are told. This indeed is a prime example of ambition without much foresight.

I'll predict that the madcap rush to AI self-driving cars is going to hit its own speedbumps. The early versions, when unleashed upon the world prematurely, will likely get involved in accidents or maybe even cause accidents. There will be a backlash about how this could have been allowed. Foresight will suddenly come into vogue. Hindsight will open the eyes of some to the need for appropriate aspects of safety to be considered, but done in a manner that does not crush the ambitions.

Yep, this is a good lesson for us to definitely keep in mind.

Frankenstein Lesson #4: Assuming that someone else will take responsibility can lead to irresponsibility

In the story of Frankenstein, one might argue that Victor shrugs off his responsibility at first for the "monster" he has created. Things just regrettably turned out a bad way, but not due to his fault, so he believes (falsely). This is a form of either passive ethics or downright ethical neglect.

For AI self-driving cars, one question that is still being grappled with involves who will take responsibility for AI self-driving cars.

Up until the vaunted Level 5, it is considered that the human driver in the self-driving car has responsibility for whatever happens with the self-driving car. But, for the Level 5, presumably there is no human driver and therefore no human in the car to be held responsible for what the car does. This has led to much debate about things like car insurance, since today we always enforce that the human driver carries the car insurance.

Will we expect the auto maker to be responsible for the acts of the AI self-driving car? Suppose the auto maker did not make the AI system and bought it from some other company. Will the auto maker be blameless and only the other company be responsible? Or, are they co-joined in responsibility. Some rather nutty (in my humble opinion) pundits have said that the AI holds the responsibility. This assumes that the AI is the equivalent of a human and has its own independent being, which, I can tell, it will be a long, long, long time from now before that happens (if ever).

If you are using a ride sharing AI self-driving car, maybe the ride sharing company has responsibility for the self-driving car. Some say that maybe the government should be responsible for self-driving cars, perhaps by some kind of governmental sponsored car insurance for self-driving cars.

Anyway, it is all of valid consideration in that per the lesson from Frankenstein, we don't want to end-up with finger pointing and no one taking responsibility for AI self-driving cars and what they do, and so pursuits to pin down that responsibility are indeed worthwhile.

Frankenstein Lesson #5: Hubris can produce self-delusions and lead to bad consequences

In the story of Frankenstein, Victor appears to exhibit a great deal of hubris. He's sure he can bring something to life. Come heck or high water, he'll be able to do it. This can cloud one's thinking. Victor doesn't even consider that the creation could go bad. An overconfident inventor such as Victor assumes boastfully that they can always undo what they have done. They have the power to giveth, and they can taketh, as they see fit.

As mentioned earlier about AI self-driving cars, some worry that our hubris as technologists causes us to assume that no matter what might have bad consequences with self-driving cars, we can easily overcome any such issues with a few lines of code.

Suppose an AI self-driving car goes berserk and runs down a bunch of pedestrians, no problem, in that we just update the artificial neural network and pump it down into those offending self-driving cars. Good as new.

There is definitely a lot of hubris going on right now in the self-driving car industry.

In one sense, the auto makers and tech firms are in a self-driving car "arms race" wherein society has now politically forced them into exhibiting hubris. These firms and developers need to convince the marketplace that a true AI self-driving car is just around the corner in terms of being invented. They need to brush away any criticism about the pell-mell rush underway. The slightest hint of ratcheting down the hubris would be perceived as a sign that these firms aren't going to be able to produce Level 5 self-driving cars. This could cause share prices of those auto makers and tech firms to drop. This could cause shareholders to revolt. This could cause heads to roll.

As I've predicted repeatedly, once we see AI self-driving cars getting into actual accidents and having real-world difficulties, it will turn the tide on the hubris. Hubris will lose its badge of honor.

Remember when the automobile industry started to acknowledge that you could get hurt in cars, and then the advertising shifted toward safety features of cars. Until then, no auto maker talked about their safety features, since it was a taboo topic. Why bring up something that will simple make people think about the dangers of being in cars. But, then it became a mad rush to see which auto maker could claim they had the safest cars and the most safety features.

I'd be willing to bet that's what will happen with the AI self-driving car industry. The unwritten rules of the race right now involves being the first out the gate with a true self-driving car. The next race will be as to which auto maker or tech firm is doing the most to ensure that their self-driving cars are safest and have the most safety features. We aren't there yet, and it will take a shift in the mindset and marketplace to get there.

I liken this to earthquakes. Nobody cares much about earthquake insurance and earthquake preparedness, until an actual earthquake hits. I am just hoping that we don't need to suffer a massive earthquake in the self-driving car industry to get us all more toward the crucial considerations surrounding self-driving car safety.

Conclusion

I hope that these Frankenstein lessons were thought provoking for you. The goal would be to spark an already budding dialogue about the nature of AI self-driving cars and the social impacts of these "creations" (let's use the word "creations" and not call them monsters, at least not yet!). Mary Shelley has provided us with a rich source of universal questions about the nature of mankind. In the same manner that the Frankenstein creation was not really a monster per se, certainly not at first launch, we are in a good place now at the infancy of AI self-driving cars to consider what we will do now, doing so in order to forge a better future for us all.

I truly believe that we can bring together the inventor-needed qualities of ambition, hubris, obsession, and other facets that will achieve this remarkable innovation, and yet do so without suffering from the dark underbelly of irresponsibility, and abandonment consequences, and the like.

Admittedly, there are some pessimists that paint a bleak picture in that they say that with great things must always come great adverse consequences, implying that the two are inextricably intertwined and there's nothing we can do to get one without the other. I'd like to think that's not the case.

Let's keep pushing forward on AI self-driving cars, and do so with the perspective that we can prevent our own creations from destroying us. Ban the Frankencars and don't allow a Level 6 -- let's all work together to get AI self-driving cars that enhance mankind, rather than allowing them to undermine mankind. That's the kind of creation we want

CHAPTER 10
OMNIPRESENCE
FOR
SELF-DRIVING CARS

Lance B. Eliot

CHAPTER 10

OMNIPRESENCE
FOR
SELF-DRIVING CARS

In my college days, we used to drive from Los Angeles up to the Bay Area so that we could watch our football team play against several of our most bitter rivals. The driving time was about six to seven hours and was quite a journey. Me and my college buddies would pile into several cars and act like a caravan for the driving journey. Whomever was at the front of the pack of cars would let the rest of us know whether there was anything up ahead to be mindful of.

The ad hoc news provided to us by the lead car included aspects of the utmost importance, such as a speed trap being maintained by the California Highway Patrol up ahead (we certainly didn't want to get caught speeding!), and encompassed rather mundane aspects such as a herd of cows a few miles in front of us that we'd be able to see off to the right in some grazing pasture. Notably, sometimes the updates were quite crucial safety tips – I remember one time that the lead car saw a couch fall off the back of a pick-up truck and alerted the rest of us to be on the watch for it, as it was sitting in the middle lanes of the highway and could have caused any of us to get into a dreadful car wreck.

We'd usually start the journey and be just a few car lengths away from each other, therefore the news items weren't much of a heads-up since we could see what the cars ahead of us saw. But, after about an hour of driving, we'd all invariably get spread out. The lead car might be a few miles ahead, and the last car in the caravan might be several miles behind the next-to-last car in the sequence. You'd maybe think that only the lead car would have something useful or significant to say, but that's not only the case. One time, the trailing car notified the rest of us that a motorcade of police was barreling along on the highway at a very high speed and rushing past him and would likely catch-up with the rest of us and the lead car in maybe fifteen minutes at the speed they were going.

I admit that this was in an era before we had GPS readily available and there wasn't Google Maps and nor specialized apps like Waze. Today, those kinds of handy tools provide helpful traffic related information and are often essential for navigating the roadways. Those tools do a good job of providing insights about the roads, but they still aren't quite fully all-encompassing. If you are driving on a road that has a tight curve up ahead, none of those apps will necessarily in real-time at the moment that you need to know be able to tell you that there's a car that just stalled there about thirty seconds ago, and if you take the curve tightly you might ram into it. Only once you've started into the curve will you realize what's afoot, and hopefully have the driving skills to avert a dangerous situation.

What does this have to do with AI self-driving cars?

At the Cybernetic Self-Driving Car Institute, we are working on helping to make self-driving cars more savvy about roadway conditions in real-time so that they will be better prepared during actual journeys on the roadways.

Some have wondered whether AI self-driving cars will be able to tap into GPS, Google Maps, Waze, and other such tools to help navigate the roadways. Yes, by-and-large, most of the auto makers and tech firms that are developing self-driving cars are making provisions to utilize those kinds of tools. That's relatively straightforward and there's not much trickery or special capabilities needed to tap into those info sources and use them.

One step even further though involves trying to make AI self-driving cars essentially omnipresent.

Now, I realize that this is not the divine kind of omnipresence, and some are maybe even a bit offended at the use of the word omnipresent being used in this context. Excuse the use of the word, and please go along with the overall meaning or spirit of what the word entails. Allow me a moment to explain.

The notion is that self-driving cars will be able to communicate with each other, and too the roadway infrastructure, doing so in a manner that they will each be able to warn or inform the others about real-time roadway conditions.

In a sense, it's kind of like how me and my buddies would provide updates during our caravan trips. A self-driving car ahead of my self-driving car might communicate to my self-driving car that it has just observed a stalled car at the curve ahead of me, which it already passed through, and so now my AI will be forewarned as to the stalled car. The AI of my self-driving car will presumably change how it was going to take the curve, since it now knows that the stalled car might well be stuck there and could get rammed into.

There is a large push toward V2V (vehicle-to-vehicle) communications going on in the car industry right now. You can do V2V to any kind of car, whether a human driven car or a self-driving car, though certainly the self-driving car to another self-driving car is going to be the most seamless way of communicating about driving conditions. Similar to my earlier point, the AI of a self-driving car ahead of you might via V2V communicate to the AI of your self-driving car about a vehicle that is stalled on the curve ahead. Or, maybe it warns you about a couch that's sitting in the middle of the highway ahead of you. And so on.

Besides V2V, there is also V2I (vehicle-to-infrastructure), which involves cars that communicate with the roadway infrastructure. For example, a bridge up ahead of me might have one of the lanes closed due to an accident that happened on the bridge, and so the bridge itself communicates to my car to let me know about the situation. The other day there was a flooded street near where I live, and I only found out once I turned onto the street and there was an electronic board sign displaying a message to turn back. It would have been more helpful if the electronic board sign was broadcasting an electronic message to nearby cars to let them know well in-advance of getting onto the street. This would have avoided having tons of cars that were all trying frantically to make U-turns.

There's also V2P, which is somewhat controversial, and refers to vehicle-to-pedestrian communication. This would allow pedestrians to communicate out to cars, and likewise for cars to communicate to pedestrians. For example, the other day there was a school that was walking several classes over to a nearby store, and the young students were all trying to cross the streets. A teacher that was guiding the students could have used a pedestrian electronic link to let nearby cars know that children were crossing the street and to therefore drive with extra caution.

Some argue that having pedestrians communicating with cars is fraught with issues. Suppose a pedestrian tries to trick cars into not driving on a particular street and so the pedestrian sends a message that a six-hundred-pound gorilla is standing in the middle of that particular street (well, maybe not a gorilla, but you know what I mean, someone making a false claim to discourage car traffic).

This does bring up the whole topic of trustworthiness in any of these kinds of communications, whether it be V2V, V2I, or V2P (the collective set of such communications is called V2X). Just because a car up ahead of you says there is a couch in the middle of the roadway, why should you believe it? Maybe the car up ahead is trying to trick other cars. Or, maybe the car up ahead truly believes there is a couch there, but there isn't one. For the V2I, we would likely hope that the infrastructure would be more trustworthy since it likely is being maintained by a governmental agency, rather than a car-to-car communication which might be coming from just anybody.

Another important factor is the timeliness of the communications. If a V2V takes place, and the self-driving car ahead of you is let's say completely truthful, and it says that there is a stalled car around the curve, you need to weigh the timing of the communication. Suppose the self-driving car that's ahead of you had sent that message just now, but that it was based on having driven through that the curve twenty minutes ago. Perhaps by now the stalled car is no longer there. Your self-driving car might be using information that is outdated, and therefore take actions that are no longer needed or appropriate.

On the topic of timeliness, when I drove down that flooded street later that night, I noticed that the electronic sign board was still saying that the street was flooded. But, by nighttime, the waters had receded, and the street was just fine. Obviously, the street maintenance crew had left the electronic board sign there and had neglected to change the message or remove the sign itself. This is another example of the timeliness of information, and in this case imagine if the V2I was broadcast to cars that the street was flooded. Thus, even if we consider V2I to potentially be more trustworthy, it's going to be vulnerable to lack of timeliness and other undermining factors.

So, we want self-driving cars to know what's around the next corner and beyond its horizon, but we also know that getting such information can be difficult, plus knowing whether the information is timely and accurate is definitely a concern. If we're aiming for some kind of true omnipresence, the self-driving car and its AI have to be aware of the real-world and not fall for fakery, ill will, or other adverse aspects.

As an example of how extreme things could get, imagine a criminal that had robbed a bank and wants to have a clear path for a getaway. They could have their self-driving car tell other nearby cars that traffic is clogged up and those cars should avoid the congestion by going down a different street. This could open the roadway for the getaway car. And, if done really cleverly, maybe even block the police that might be coming down that other street into which traffic is now heading. I realize this seems like a plot in a bad science fiction movie, but I am just pointing out that we'll need to have safeguards that take these kinds of aspects into account.

How can the AI of the self-driving car know whom to trust?

One viewpoint is that the AI should be weighing the sources of the data and give more or less weight to various sources. The V2I might have a high weighting, while the V2V might have a lower weighting since it is considered less trustworthy. If the V2V is coming from a police car or official government vehicle, perhaps the weighting goes to high.

Another aspect involves comparing multiple sources. If there are a lot of V2V's happening all at once, and if the preponderance of them are saying there's a couch in the middle of the highway, this would be considered more likely as being a real report versus if only one other car made such a claim. The idea is to use crowdsourcing as a method and via voting or other conflict measurements try to ascertain what's true versus what is not.

This brings up another facet of these communications, namely how many of them can your self-driving car handle at once? Suppose that there are a hundred other self-driving cars around you, and all of them are bombarding your AI with what's going on. Second by second, or maybe even much faster, such as every millisecond. Meanwhile, let's suppose that the roadway infrastructure has dozens of broadcasting sites near your self-driving car as it is traveling along on the highway. How does your self-driving car decide which of these sources to give attention to? Trying to decipher all of them at once might be daunting and consume a tremendous amount of on-board processing and memory. Right now, we have so few of V2X in place that it is an easy task for an experimental self-driving car to cope with, but once we have lots of V2V, V2I, and V2P, it will be a deluge of data, some of which is useful and some not, some of which is timely and some not, etc.

Notice that I've been describing the communications as though the information conveyed is crisply stated and summarized, but it doesn't have to be that way. The data could be raw data coming from another self-driving car's cameras or radar or other sensors. In that case, the self-driving car that receives the data would be able to analyze and interpret it, rather than relying upon the interpretation provided by the other self-driving car. The downside with interpreting it would include the time needed by the receiving self-driving car to do so, plus it might not be familiar with the type of camera images or radar data that is being provided (the other self-driving car might be using a different make or model than the sensors on the receiving self-driving car).

This brings up the aspect that we'll need some universal protocols for the V2V, V2I, V2P, which are indeed being formulated, along with how to interpret the data. In addition, the data needs to be timestamped so that if there's a delay during communicating, the receiving self-driving cars will know that the data is time lagged.

The time lag could be crucial in life-or-death circumstances. If the self-driving car ahead of me has just rammed into another car, and if my self-driving car has not detected the crash, and meanwhile the self-driving car involved in the crash has sent out a message, we need to consider how long will it take for the message to be emitted and received. Suppose the V2V is occurring by use of the Internet, and so the self-driving car in the crash sends out a message across the Internet, and assuming that there is a link, and assuming that my self-driving car also has a connection to the Internet, it could take a lot longer than the time it takes for my car that's going 80 miles per hour to pile into the crashing cars.

It would also likely be beneficial to classify messages that are going to be sent back-and-forth. A message that offers a danger ahead warning of an impending accident scene would seem to be more important than a message that says the road ahead has some minor potholes. Messages should be conveyed as to whether the indications are of an immediate concern or an overall concern, and how much priority should be given to the message.

Another question involves whether all self-driving cars are going to be required to send and receive messages, or whether you can opt out of having your self-driving car participate. Maybe you don't want your self-driving car to send messages, and only receive messages. Maybe you only want to send messages, but not receive messages. Or, perhaps you don't think any kind of messaging should be undertaken by your self-driving car. Will we as a society require that messaging occur or allow it to be voluntary?

Furthermore, will the messages be attributable to a vehicle? In other words, maybe the messages should be sent anonymously to allow for privacy. But, some would say that anonymous messages would lend itself to people sending trick messages and not taking things seriously. There are those that believe that your self-driving car should be sending messages and should also be saying that it is the one sending the messages, thus allowing for being able to trace where the messages came from. We could use some kind of specialized ID that your self-driving car emits but is only known as being your self-driving car by getting a court order. These kinds of arrangements though have various downsides and trade-offs.

Some believe that our self-driving cars will be able to build-up trustworthiness over time. Let's pretend that your self-driving car has reported one hundred valuable roadway aspects, and so it is considered a more trustworthy source of roadway info. Some say that we might even setup micropayments, whereby self-driving cars that the owners opt to have participate in messaging will get paid to do so. Or, maybe it will be ad based. Or, some think the government should compensate those that allow their self-driving cars to aid in traffic management.

If you're interested in the topic of data exchange between vehicles and also roadside infrastructure, you ought to take a look at the Wireless Access in Vehicular Environments (WAVE) standard. The standard and the IEEE 802.11p are part of the set of various protocols that are being developed and fielded for these V2X purposes. This also includes VANETS, Vehicular Ad-hoc Networks, and the use of DSRC's (Dedicated Short-Range Communications). The infrastructure would have RSU's, RoadSide Units, which are doing the broadcasting.

Some vendors and developers are pushing forward on the omnipresence goal. For example, an Australian company called Cohda has been developing systems for "surround vision" using Nvidia's Drive platform. Their hope is to further provide 360-degree awareness for AI self-driving cars, allowing any self-driving car to essentially see around the bend by collecting and synthesizing data from other nearby self-driving cars.

With the advent of 5G mobile networks, we'll gradually have the needed speed to try and ensure that the communications are happening on a timely enough basis.

As mentioned, some of the most limiting factors involve connectivity issues, bandwidth constraints, signal fading, routing aspects, and the like. Furthermore, there are some quite serious privacy issues that arise, along with crucial security considerations. Imagine if a terrorist were able to break into the omnipresence and broadcast messages that misled self-driving cars into taking dangerous actions.

One last aspect to consider involves whether the communications should also include advice from the communicating source. Suppose a self-driving car up ahead reports that there's a couch in the middle of the roadway. This is informative to my self-driving car, which then the AI decides what to do. If the self-driving car ahead had also suggested that other cars behind it should get off the highway, would this be helpful or not to the receiving self-driving cars. It might be helpful in that maybe that's the right thing to do. Or, it might be misleading or even distracting and not be a prudent step to take. It's one thing to say what is occurring or what is detected, and its another to then make a recommendation or stated action for others to take.

In whatever manner this all plays out, there's no doubting that we'll ultimately have V2V, V2I, V2P, and the technology will be developed sufficiently to allow it to occur. The rules of how it is to be used, and what it is to be used for, will require not just a technological perspective, but also require a societal, political, business, and ethical perspective. We're still in the infancy of these capabilities and it's timely to start laying a foundation for what this will become. Omnipresence should be aimed at being a good thing, and not be allowed to fall into something that is ill-used and that endangers our roadway safety.

CHAPTER 11

LOOKING BEHIND YOU

FOR

SELF-DRIVING CARS

CHAPTER 11

LOOKING BEHIND YOU
FOR SELF-DRIVING CARS

In college, my roommate was a car buff. He loved cars. Whenever he had the time, he would tinker with some aspect of his beloved car. At first, I thought he knew everything thing there was to know about cars. He did though have some quirks, one of which I discovered during a first-time ride with him in his pampered car. I had noticed while sitting in the passenger seat that he rarely seemed to look at his rear-view mirror. Upon closer inspection, I realized that there wasn't a mirror in his rear-view mirror.

I asked him why he did not have a mirror in his rear-view mirror. This seemed to me like a "glaring" omission that should be rectified right away. In other words, the rear-view mirror structure was mounted in the normal spot on the front windshield, but there wasn't a glass mirror inside the rear-view mirror. It was mirrorless. He then explained to me that this was done on purpose. What, I asked incredulously, could be the purpose for having a rear-view mirror that is mirrorless?

His answer: There's no reason for him to look behind himself.

Huh? This seemed to be an answer that itself was also a mystery. Why would he not need to look behind his car? He said that it was because anyone that was behind his car had the responsibility to not get in his way, and he didn't therefore envision any bona fide reason to need to look behind himself.

Note that he "cleverly" and purposely had not removed the rear-view mirror mount itself due to it legally being required by the Department of Motor Vehicles (DMV) that he had to have one. He didn't want to get a ticket from a cop and so he figured no one would ever know that he didn't have the actual mirror in the rear-view mirror. Thus, he had a rear-view mirror that he never needed to glance at and it was there solely for ornamental purposes to avoid getting fined.

I pointed out that I was pretty sure that if a cop realized there wasn't a mirror he would still get a ticket, in spite of having the mount. He said that the odds of a cop realizing that there wasn't a mirror was slim, and if a cop did realize it, the issued ticket would only be a fix-it ticket that would be easy to rectify. Seemed amazing to me that he had put so much effort into this, when he could have just left the darned mirror in the thing.

This kind of boggles the mind and is pretty wild. A driver that does not believe he or she needs to look behind themselves. No need to see the traffic behind them. Just drive forward and anything behind you will need to take care of itself. Life is apparently forward looking, not backward looking.

Where else do we see this kind of logic? In some of today's self-driving cars.

That's right, some of today's self-driving cars do not seem to be worried about looking behind the car. At the Cybernetics Self-Driving Car Institute, we are expanding the capabilities of self-driving cars to appropriately utilize awareness of what is behind the car.

You might be saying to yourself that most cars already now have a back-up cam, and indeed it is gradually becoming a mandated feature on American cars, thus they can "see" behind themselves. A back-up cam though is just used for backing up, when you are moving relatively slowly, and in reverse. It is not used when you are moving forward. Tesla's have a radar unit on the front grill of the car, but no radar at the back of the car. They have cameras pointing at the back on the Model 3, but no other sensory devices for this purpose.

Why would you care about what's behind your car?

Well, imagine that you are sitting at an intersection due to a red light and a car coming up behind you is coming at you very quickly. Your judgement tells you that the wayward car is going to ram into the rear of your car. You quickly move out of the way to avoid getting crashed into. This happened to me a few months ago. I did a risky safety maneuver by going into the intersection (luckily it was open) to avoid the careless car that was coming upon me – presumably the driver and had not realized that the light was red. Had I not moved out of the way, it would have been smash city. If I hadn't been looking at my rear-view mirror, I would not have known to move out of the way.

For most starting drivers such as teenagers, they are instructed to always be checking their rear-view mirror. Glance at it frequently. Know what cars are behind you. Know how fast they are moving. Know if they are directly behind you, or whether they are in a different lane. Be aware of your surroundings. Be watching for motorcyclists that are coming up behind you. Indeed, during my morning commute on the freeway, I often see cars ahead of me that have realized a motorcycle is coming up upon them, and it is weaving throughout traffic as it cuts on the lane lines. Those observant drivers that are watching their rear-view mirror move over slightly from the lane line to give the motorcyclist a little added space to pass. It is a courtesy and also a means to reduce the chances that the motorcyclist will hit their car.

Most of the motorcyclist accidents that I witness on the freeway are typically due to a car driver that did not realize the motorcycle was coming up behind them. Whether the human driver was lazy or just being forgetful, they made a lane change and plowed right into a motorcyclist. Believe it or not, this happens about once per week during my five days a week freeway commute. Over and over again, I see a car make a lane change and a motorcyclist that gets caught going forward and ramming into the lane switching car. Did the driver of the car look in their rear-view mirror to see what was behind them? Probably not.

We expect teenage drivers to be using their rear-view mirrors whenever they make a lane change. The recommended practice by the DMV involves first checking your rear-view mirror, and then looking over your shoulder as a double-check that its clear to make the lane change, along with using your side-view mirrors. Suppose we told a teenage driver they did not need to look in their rear-view mirror, they did not need to look at their side-view mirrors, and they did not need to look over their shoulder. I believe you would likely agree we'd have chaos and accidents aplenty.

This is what we're going to also experience with many self-driving cars, until the self-driving car makers get more in-tune with considering what goes on behind a car. Self-driving cars equipped with LIDAR are fortunately able to "see" behind the car. By using laser pulses, the LIDAR can potentially identify objects behind the car. I say the word potentially because this assumes that the LIDAR is being used for a 360-degree perspective around the car. Some LIDAR have a narrower Field of Vision (FOV) and do not encompass a full 360-degree viewpoint. Even the ones that do have a 360-degree FOV are often programmed to not be especially mindful of what is behind the car.

Let me explain this a bit further in terms of what is technically going on. The LIDAR that is able to collect a 360-degree view is simply gathering data. It is up to whatever AI component is doing sensor fusion to figure out what the data actually means. If the AI system is programmed to not utilize the data from the LIDAR that shows what is happening behind the car, it makes little difference that the LIDAR is collecting it at all. This is equivalent to having a teenage driver that looks in their rear-view mirror, sees what is going on behind their car, but is unable to mentally process this visualization and just proceeds to drive as though they really hadn't looked at the rear-view mirror at all.

Why wouldn't an AI system make sure to squeeze every ounce of data from the LIDAR? It could be that the developers didn't realize that using rearward data would be important. They might have thought the same thing that my college roommate believed, namely that having data from behind you isn't particularly important. Or, they might have been rushed to develop the AI for the self-driving car and didn't have the time or resources to develop code to analyze rearward data. One might also consider that processing the rearward data takes processing power and so you need to have more processors on the self-driving car to do this kind of calculating. It can be a cost factor of having more processors and so therefore it increases the cost of the self-driving car. Another possibility is that the rearward data is only analyzed for the most obvious of deadly circumstances, but otherwise the data is ignored.

For example, suppose a car is coming up behind you at a fast rate of speed. Let's suppose the LIDAR is detecting this object, in this case the car coming up behind you. In the virtual model of the world surrounding the self-driving car, the AI needs to figure out that the car is coming up toward the self-driving car, and it is coming up at a fast speed. Does a fast speed mean that the other car will hit the self-driving car? No, not necessarily. It could be that the other car will change lanes, sometimes at the last moment, and avoid rear-ending into the self-driving car. Some AI programmers assume that the other car is being driven in a rationale way and that "obviously" the other driver will make sure to avoid hitting the self-driving car.

This belies the fact that every day we have thousands of rear-end accidents taking place. The rearward data should be used to make predictions about what might happen. Each day, during my morning commute, I am mentally calculating whether a car rushing up behind me will potentially ram into my car. If I think the risk factor is high enough, I take evasive action. We should expect that our self-driving cars should use the same logic.

Self-driving cars should be collecting rearward data, they should be merging it within the virtual model of their surroundings, and they need to ascertain probabilities of potential dangers and how to drive defensively because of the dangers. Elon Musk has said that he doesn't believe that LIDAR is needed for self-driving cars. In which case, if you believe as I do that knowing what's behind you is essential for a true self-driving car, he's betting that cameras alone are sufficient for rearward inspection. Cameras have numerous limitations and so having just one kind of sensory device for rearward data collection is dicey.

Besides detecting cars that are approaching you, it is also important to keep track of pedestrians that are behind you. When I was driving down an alley last year, and though I was moving very slowly, a pedestrian walked right up behind my car and walked right into it. I admit that I had not seen him, even though I was glancing at my rear-view mirror from time-to-time. I heard a thump on the trunk of my car, and imagine my shock to look back and see that a human was bent over on the trunk of my car. I even thought at first that it was a scam. Maybe the person wanted to claim an accident had happened and get me to pay them off or maybe file an insurance claim.

But, anyway, the point is that anything can be behind a car and be something that the driver needs to know about. An approaching car, an approaching motorcyclist, an approaching pedestrian, an approaching bicyclist, an approaching skateboarder, and so on. Emergency vehicles are another category of important objects that can be approaching from behind. I fervently argue that we need to have multiple types of sensors to detect what's behind a self-driving car, and we need to have the sensor fusion and AI that well uses that information.

Due to economic reasons, self-driving car makers are tending to have just one form of sensor technology for looking rearward. Each type of sensor has its own limitations. Combining the perspective of multiple sensors is key for driving safety. To me, a true self-driving car ought to have LIDAR, cameras, and radar for rearward data collection. If we want to ultimately achieve a Level 5 self-driving car, I suggest we will need multiple types of sensors and a more rigorous effort of AI software that can stitch together the data and take appropriate actions.

Watch out for what's behind you!

CHAPTER 12
OVER-THE-AIR (OTA)
UPDATING FOR
SELF-DRIVING CARS

Lance B. Eliot

CHAPTER 12

OVER-THE-AIR (OTA) UPDATING FOR SELF-DRIVING CARS

Windows updates.

You are probably like me in that when you see that it's time to install Windows updates to your PC it is a moment of internal angst and overall distress.

I am betting this flashes through your mind:

- Should you go ahead and let the updates be installed, or would you be safer to avoid accepting the updates
- What is going to be installed and do you really want or need whatever changes that Microsoft thinks you should have?
- Will it possibly change features into becoming something incomprehensible and that you'll then have to begrudgingly learn anew how to use?
- How long will it take for the updates to get installed and will you need to walk away from your PC and go make a pot of coffee or play a game of cards until it eventually and painstakingly is completed?
- Suppose you start the install and want to stop it – can you do so midstream or will it toast your PC?

Speaking of which, you likely wonder too what the odds are that even if the install completes, whether it might "brick" your system (an expression meaning cause your PC to become unusable like a brick).

Now, in spite of the above downsides of the updating process, it admittedly is handy that you can do updates nowadays via the Internet and not have to get a CD or DVD that you'd need to insert into your PC and run the installs from there. Furthermore, it's kind of handy that your system can automatically do the updates without you necessarily needing to enter any elaborate commands or have to remember on your own when to do an update. Instead, the system alerts you when updates are needed and does all the heavy lifting of installing the updates.

What does this have to do with AI self-driving cars, you might be asking?

At the Cybernetic Self-Driving Car Institute, we are working on the Over-The-Air (OTA) capabilities for updating the AI of self-driving cars.

You might already be aware that Tesla is known for having an over-the-air capability. Similar in some respects as the aforementioned Windows updates for a PC, a Tesla can do updates via having the updates pumped down into your Tesla car, doing so remotely. In other words, no need to take your car into a dealership and have them physically connect to your Tesla to provide software updates. Instead, you can via an online connection do the updates wherever you happen to have an online connection available.

Cool.

Indeed, one of the touted advantages for self-driving cars involves this OTA capability. For the software that runs your self-driving car, you can get all sorts of updates as needed, whenever needed, wherever needed. This means too that your self-driving car can nearly "instantly" get any of the newest features that the auto maker wants to provide to you. It all seems great and glorious.

To a degree, it is a boon for those that will be owning and using AI self-driving cars. But, as with most things in life, there are also some downsides and aspects to be considered in this expected glory.

Some predictions are that by the year 2022, there will be potentially 160 million vehicles that will have some form of OTA. Now, this does not mean they will all be self-driving cars. Nor are these even going to necessarily be true self-driving cars for those that are self-driving cars – note that there are levels of self-driving cars, with Level 5 being the highest and considered a true self-driving car, one that is driven by the AI in the same manner that a human could drive the car and thus no human driver is needed.

The OTA capability is handy for even non-self-driving cars in that for any kind of software or data that is being used within your car that it can be updated readily via an OTA capability. Therefore, please don't think that the OTA is solely for self-driving cars. It's not. Your car might have a cruise control capability that is marginally a self-driving version, but that is performed by software stored in processors on-board your conventional car, and for which updates to that software to presumably improve the cruise control could readily be undertaken via an OTA capability of your conventional car.

Most of the auto makers realize that having an OTA capability is handy for any conventional car, and especially so too for self-driving cars, and so it is gradually going to become a standard feature on all cars. The OTA capability consists of having some kind of communications device on-board the car, and that connects to other components of the car, so that after getting updates across the communications line that then the car can update the internal components accordingly.

Notice this means that the car needs to be designed for this purpose. If the components of the car weren't designed to be able to get updates, it does little good to have a communications device to get updates. Likewise, if the components of the car were designed to be updated, but if there isn't a communications device to receive updates then it's all for naught. Even if you have the right kinds of internal components and the right kind of communication device, you are obviously dependent on the ability to actually communicate via the communications device.

Currently, when you do a Windows update to your PC, you've maybe had the experience of Windows opting to do a many mega-bytes update but that you were on a WiFi that was low-speed. I'm betting that it took seemingly forever to get the updates downloaded to your PC. This is the same potential problem for OTA on a car. If the communications device is connecting via WiFi, and if your WiFi network is slow, it could take a long time to get the updates downloaded to your car.

I mention this aspect because the earlier idealized notion of OTA allowing for updates at any time, and at any place, becomes a bit more murky because you need to be in a place where you have a sufficient communications connection to actually get the updates downloaded. If your self-driving car is parked in your garage at home, does your WiFi extend to and include your garage area? Is it a strong connection or a weak connection? Suppose you self-driving car is elsewhere and driving around, will there be any WiFi connection you could use? As you can see, it might be problematic to find a good spot and a solid connection for getting the OTA updates.

Let's take a closer look at how Tesla handles their OTA for their Model S, which is handy as an exemplar. I am not picking on Tesla, and nor nitpicking Tesla, and merely using this as an example for purposes of illustrative discussion.

From the Tesla Manual

According to the Model S owner's manual:

"Model S updates its software wirelessly, providing new features throughout your term of ownership."

Notice that they've said that the updates are performed wirelessly, which is via their OTA, and they also interestingly state that you can get the updates through your term of ownership. This would seem to suggest that if you transfer ownership of the car to someone else, you no longer are able to get the updates, which I suppose one could say is comparable to if Microsoft allowed you licensed updates for your Windows operating system and did so as long as you were the owner of it.

Suggestion: Be aware of what your OTA licensing rights are when you buy your AI self-driving car.

Next, here's more of what the Model S owner's manual says:

"Tesla recommends that you install software updates as soon as they are available."

This suggests that you should right away make sure to OTA the updates. Of course, as mentioned earlier, you might not be able to do so due to not being in a time or place conducive to do the updates.

We'll hope and suppose that by-and-large you'll be safe driving your self-driving car even if you have not yet done the updates, but admittedly it's one thing to be unsure about having your Windows PC at home updated or not, versus driving around in an AI self-driving car that maybe needs updates that involve life-or-death changes and you've not yet been able to make the updates.

This is one of the downsides generally about the OTA. If it provides something essential to the safety and well-being of the AI self-driving car and its human occupants, having potential delays in using the OTA to make the updates could have some very serious consequences.

Here's some more from the Model S owner's manual:

"The first time you enter Model S after an update is made available, a scheduling window displays on the touchscreen. The scheduling window displays again at the end of your first driving session."

One aspect about the OTA is how you as the owner or occupant in an AI self-driving car will even be aware that an update is needed. With a Windows PC, you usually nowadays get a message that pops up on your Windows screen. With an AI self-driving car, the question arises as to how you are to be best notified. In the case of the Model

S, the manual says that a scheduling window will display on your touchscreen.

Here's a question for you. If owners of AI self-driving cars are going to be using their self-driving cars for ride sharing purposes, and suppose a human occupant is in the car, will we be expecting that human occupant to go ahead and take care of doing an OTA update? I wouldn't think that we'd be anticipating that to happen. Presumably, it's something the car owner should be taking care of. But, suppose the car owner never even uses the self-driving car themselves, and always rents it out to others. Maybe the owner won't even be aware that an OTA is needed. I am suggesting that ultimately the OTA's on AI self-driving cars will probably need to be setup to alert humans via additional means, such as maybe the owner gets an alert on their smartphone that one of their self-driving cars needs an OTA update.

It is envisioned too that AI self-driving cars are going to be engaging human occupants in a verbal dialogue. When you get into a self-driving car, it will talk with you, asking about your desired destination, etc. It would seem likely that the self-driving car would also then possibly engage in a verbal discussion about the need for an OTA. Of course, this must be done sensibly, since if for example a child gets into the self-driving car because the car is going to give the child a lift to school, and if the child says yes go ahead and do the OTA update, we might want instead that an adult would be making such a decision.

Here's more from the owner's manual:

"Note: Some software updates can take up to three hours to complete."

Now, this statement seems a bit curious. One must wonder how an estimate of the amount of time to do an update was determined. It says "up to three hours" which seems like a gutsy statement. If it said that it could take up to three or more hours, that seems to cover circumstances wherein the WiFi is really slow and the update is really big. But the suggestion that it would never take more than three hours, which is implied, seems somewhat unknowable beforehand. Even if they opt to chop the updates into bite sized pieces to try and keep under the three hours, it still seems like a gutsy statement.

Anyway, this points out that if you were thinking that your OTA updates for your self-driving car would happen instantly, you can now see that in this case you should be thinking of perhaps several hours to do the updates. Once we have even greater complexity in AI self-driving cars, it could stretch to even much longer periods of time to do the updates.

Here's more from the owner's manual:

"Model S must be in Park while the new software is being installed."

When you do Windows updates on your PC, you often can't do anything else on the PC and must wait until the updates are done. It is likely that most AI self-driving cars are going to be designed such that you can only do updates when the self-driving car is not in motion and is otherwise in a full rested stopped position. This could be frustrating though in that suppose you start the OTA for your self-driving car and then suddenly have an emergency that requires you to want to use your self-driving car? It's not like your PC that you can just wait for it to finish.

Here's more from the manual:

"To ensure the fastest and most reliable delivery of software updates, leave the Wi-Fi turned on and connected whenever possible."

At first glance, it might seem sensible to want to leave your Wi-Fi turned on all the time so that your software updates can occur whenever possible. But, this raises other issues such as suppose you are paying for the Wi-Fi and you suddenly rack-up a large charge because your self-driving car opted to use the connection but you weren't aware it was doing so. Another concern would be security in that if you leave your Wi-Fi on all the time, it might connect to something nefarious that then digs into the innards of your self-driving car.

Here's another item from the manual:

"If the Model S is charging when the software update begins, charging stops. Charging resumes automatically when the software update is complete."

Let's suppose you park your self-driving car in your garage and it's an electric car, so you plug it into your at-home charger. Meanwhile, you also approve to do the OTA updates. In this design, suppose your updates take three hours, and as you can see your car charging will be stopped. You might come out to use your self-driving car just after three hours, and there's not as much charge in it as you assumed. Now, I realize you are supposed to be aware that your self-driving car won't be charging during updates, but it would be an easy item to have forgotten about or not even realized was the case.

Here's this from the manual:

"If you are driving Model S at the scheduled update time, the update is canceled and you need to reschedule it. You can then either: • Schedule the update by setting the time you want the update to begin. Then touch Set For This Time. Once scheduled, the yellow clock icon changes to a white clock icon. You can reschedule the update any time before it begins. OR • Touch Install Now to immediately start the update process."

This aspect is all about the scheduling of your OTA updates. It's one of those aspects that a human could mess-up on. Suppose you thought you'd be parked at work for the morning and so you scheduled the update to occur. But, while at work, you suddenly realize you need urgently to drive over to the school because your child got hurt on the playground. You jump into your self-driving car, the update cancels automatically. You completely forget that you were doing the update. And, whatever amount was undertaken might not count and you'll need to start it over again.

Here's this:

"Note: Over time, the touchscreen may display a software update window informing you to SET FOR THIS TIME or INSTALL NOW. This software update window will persist until you complete the installation of the software update."

Have you ever been to someone's house and their clocks are blinking because they had a power outage and they never reset the clocks? This could kind of happen with your AI self-driving car, in that suppose you interrupted an OTA update and didn't finish it. You might thereafter just ignore the indication to do the software update. With your Windows PC updates, maybe you'd be missing out on some nifty new feature in Word or Powerpoint, but with an AI self-driving car suppose it's a software update that fixes a bug in the braking system that cause it to not engage properly.

Here's this:

"You must install all software updates as soon as they are available and any harm relating to the failure to install a software update will not be covered by the vehicle's warranty. Failure or refusal to install such updates may result in the inaccessibility of certain vehicle features (including incompatibility with digital media devices) or in Tesla being unable to diagnose and service your vehicle."

If you forget to make your OTA updates, or you decide not to do them, what's the penalty? Well, the auto maker can say that if you don't do the OTA updates you aren't covered by the warranty. This has some teeth, but maybe not that much for some people. The auto maker can say that some features might not work as intended or have other issues. Will this be sufficient to compel people to run their OTA updates? Maybe not.

The point being that for AI self-driving cars, the aspect of OTA's being kind of optional and having soft penalties might not be enough to ensure the safety of humans. How many people for example today ignore recalls and don't get the needed recall aspects undertaken? A lot. This is indicative that we might need to have more forceful ways of ensuring that OTA updates occur.

For example, some say that maybe an AI self-driving car should not even be willing to get underway if an OTA is pending that has a high priority safety element in it. But, it's not such an easy thing to impose. Suppose someone is near death and needs to get to the hospital, and the AI self-driving car without the OTA update could get them there, which is more important at that moment, implementing the OTA update or allowing the human to use the self-driving car for that specific need at that moment?

We also need to consider the risks to other humans besides the owner. Suppose an AI self-driving car is being used by an owner for ridesharing purposes. The owner ignores the needed OTA updates. The self-driving car gets into an accident, let's suppose due to not having the OTA updates. The self-driving car injures the occupants and hits two pedestrians. As you can see, it's not just the owner that maybe carries risks, but anyone else that comes into contact with the AI self-driving car is also potentially at risk if the OTA updates are not undertaken.

Here's this:

"Note: If software updates are not installed, some vehicle features may become inaccessible and digital media devices may become incompatible. Reverting to a previous software version is not possible. If the touchscreen displays a message indicating that a software update was not successfully completed, contact Tesla."

This points out that you cannot revert to an earlier version of the system. Have you ever done some Windows updates and it made things worse, so you opted to back-out the changes? Sometimes you can revert, sometimes not. From a design perspective, the question will be whether the AI self-driving car makers are going to make it feasible to do a revert or not. They can do so, but it often takes a lot more trickery in the software and system to allow for a revert. The logic of most developers is that why would anyone want to revert? The person or thing clearly needs the OTA updates, otherwise we would not have provided them, they would assert.

Of course, we know that sometimes the OTA updates might not work, or might have adverse unintended consequences. Maybe an update fixes a problem with the use of the camera, but meanwhile messes up aspects of using the radar of the self-driving car. You cannot assume that just because the OTA updates have presumably been tested beforehand that they will always be perfect.

Here's this:

"When a software update is complete, learn about the new features by reading the release notes. To display release notes about your current software version at any time touch the Tesla "T" at the top center of the touchscreen, then touch Release Notes. Tesla strongly recommends reading all release notes. They may contain important safety information or operating instructions regarding your Model S."

After you've done a Windows update on your home PC, how often do you read the release notes to find out what changes were made? I'd bet that most people rarely if ever read the release notes. For an AI self-driving car, the changes made might have some very important aspects of a life-and-death manner. It would seem crucial to know what those changes are.

Should the auto maker force you to read the release notes?

Well, this is problematic since whom is even supposed to be reading the release notes – the owner, the human occupants, or who? And, if there's no means to revert, you might say it makes no difference to the human anyway. Plus, the AI is presumably going to be taking care of the driving and so whatever it does is what it's going to do. That's not true though for the levels below a Level 5, in that at Levels 4 and lower there is still a human driver involved and responsible for the self-driving car. As such, there might be crucial changes in the behavior of the AI about the driving of the car that the human driver might not be aware of, and at a vital moment of decision making such as an imminent car crash, the human might not know that the self-driving car is going to be doing something that it expects the human to suddenly takeover.

Some say that the AI of the self-driving car should be good enough to make sure that it informs the human drivers as to what the release notes have to say. In other words, rather than asking a human to read the release notes, the AI should engage in a dialogue with the human driver and explain what the OTA updates were for. The AI should then interactively discuss this with the human driver, rather than just passively displaying the release notes.

Computer Security for Self-Driving Cars

Now that we've covered many of the essentials about the OTA updates, let's focus for a moment on something that raises concerns quite a bit about the OTA updates, namely the computer security of the self-driving car.

You could be letting a Trojan horse piece of malware straight into the inner workings of your self-driving car by allowing an OTA update to occur. I realize you'll say that the auto maker should have made sure that their update doesn't have any malware in it, but I assure you this is going to be a continual cat-and-mouse game. Unlike a Windows update on your PC, the consequences of a malware into your self-driving car could be quite life threatening.

There's also the Man-In-The-Middle (MITM) attacks, whereby you think that you are agreeing to do an OTA update from the auto maker, and yet someone has jumped onto your Wi-Fi and they are in-between you and the auto maker. They then secretly feed something untoward into your AI self-driving car. The auto maker might be blissfully unaware that it has happened.

Some say that the systems of the AI self-driving car should be subdivided so that no one OTA update can harm them all at once. This is a potential approach, but it also makes things more complex overall. Having numerous subsystems, each of which has its own gated wall, can be handy to try and prevent an overarching attack. It presents other issues of speed of communication between the components and their needed seamless interplay.

There are needed protocols about the OTA updates, involving security precautions, encryption, and so on. Most of the auto makers and tech firms that are developing AI self-driving cars are each reinventing the wheel about how to do their OTA updates. Some are calling for the industry to establish standards for this. Also, some believe that disclosures about the OTA capabilities need to be made known to prospective buyers, right away while even considering buying a self-driving car, and not wait until after the self-driving car has been sold. There are activists saying the government should make mandates on this, while those in the industry would often say that its best left to the industry to determine.

We also need to consider the fleet-wide impacts of OTA updates. The beauty of OTA updates is that an auto maker can send out to a million of their already-sold AI self-driving cars that those cars all need to get an urgent update. Remember that for Hurricane Irma, Tesla sent out an update to Tesla's in Florida that their batteries could go a bit further and unlocked extra battery capacity. This was to help drivers there that were trying to get away before the hurricane hit.

Sidenote: Some were confused at the time and thought that Tesla magically increased battery capacity, but the reality is that Tesla had via software previously capped the allowed use of capacity on some models because the buyer didn't pay enough to get the larger battery capacity, even though the battery capacity was there in the car all along. All this did was to increase the threshold cap. The battery was still the same battery. No magic involved.

That's an example of the beauty side of OTA's, but there's the ugliness too in that if the update is accidentally a computer virus, you've now made it really easy for that computer virus to spread into a million cars, all at once. That's a rather tempting target for any hacker or terrorist. It would delight some hackers to think that they could suddenly change a million AI self-driving cars to start blinking their headlights on-and-off to the tune of their favorite song. That's a rather benign change, and just imagine what kind of nefarious changes could be done. An entire "fleet" of AI self-driving cars could overnight become crazed monster cars that go mad and run over people and run off the road.

Generally, few are right now thinking much about this, because the percentage of cars on the roads today with OTA is relatively tiny, and the amount of the control of the car in terms of software is relatively small. Once we have AI self-driving cars that involve a large amount of software and data on-board the car itself, we'll begin to realize the impacts that OTA can have on those cars. And, once those kinds of AI self-driving cars become prevalent, we'll begin to realize the vastness of the impacts. Until then, it's not the kind of eye catching issue that will garner much attention.

Elon Musk has suggested that a "kill switch" be built into AI self-driving cars and would allow a human to use it to cut the link to any OTA connection and allow the human to regain control of the car. It's not yet clear how this might work. If the self-driving car is a Level 5, it presumably won't have any controls for the human to drive the car, and thus even if yes they hit the kill switch, the car then presumably becomes a multi-ton useful paperweight. You might say that well at least let some of the AI be active so that you can tell the self-driving car to drive you home. This is problematic because suppose you've already loaded the virus and now the AI opts to ignore your instructions and drives the car off a pier.

How would this kill switch function such that it completely disables the car from working at all? Would it be software based or hardware based? Would anyone be able to use it? Suppose a child is in the AI self-driving car and just for fun hits the kill switch? If you hit the kill switch while the car is in motion, what happens? Does the car instantly come to a halt, but maybe doing so puts you into greater jeopardy? And so on.

Besides the intentional attacks on a self-driving car by outsiders, we also need to consider the unintentional aspects. Suppose the auto maker provides an OTA update that bricks your self-driving car. Let's suppose it passes the security of the OTA and so legitimately comes into the innards of the self-driving car. I know that the auto makers often don't want to bring up this possibility, but it is a true possibility. We could also even have third-parties that offer ways to jack your self-driving car, and they provide OTA updates that you can subvert the auto maker and have directly go into your self-driving car. I am sure that if someone tells you they can make your self-driving car go faster and take turns tightly, there will be some owners of AI self-driving cars that will be willing to go off-market to get those updates.

Currently, everyone is pretty much going to assume that the OTA stuff works and works properly. Sadly, if there's not sufficient attention beforehand, we'll potentially find the self-driving car industry getting into trouble down-the-road, and all of sudden there will be the public and regulators up-in-arms as to how this came to be. Let's hope we don't get to that.

CHAPTER 13

SNOW DRIVING

FOR SELF-DRIVING CARS

Lance B. Eliot

CHAPTER 13
SNOW DRIVING
FOR SELF-DRIVING CARS

I lived in Germany for a year and "fondly" recall one of the most terrifying driving experiences in my life, which involved being on an autobahn in the middle of a snow storm.

When I left my apartment in my rented car to head out to work one day, the snow was heavy on the ground but relatively well-plowed and the roads were open. I knew to be generally cautious in driving in the snow, but didn't anticipate any special situations or predicaments that I'd need to be worried about. The skies looked ugly with the potential for some lite snow showers. This was pretty much a typical winter looking day in Frankfurt. It was certainly a drivable day and the locals all acted like the weather was not a concern at all.

After driving onto the autobahn, snow started to come down from the skies. At first, it was those cute little flakes of fluffy snow that are fun to see and that melt right away. Then, the snow started to come down like it was angry and wanted to blanket the earth in a dense and thick layer of snow. I figured that maybe if I drove fast enough, I could make it to my exit and get to work before things became really dicey. The windshield wipers on the car could not keep up with the snow and gradually I couldn't see out the windshield. I rolled down the driver side window and tried to stick my head out, hoping to see the road ahead of me.

Meanwhile, there were other determined drivers on the autobahn that were trying to pass me. Other cars were going very slowly. The snow on the road itself was piling up. A car near me began to slide and I just barely avoided getting hit. My face was freezing as I continued to use a strained neck and my head out the window to see where I was going. The whole situation had rapidly deteriorated and I was unsure of what to do. A few cars were pulling over to the side of the autobahn and parking their cars. This seemed quite dangerous as they were still on the autobahn and now parked in the so-called slow lane.

Believe it or not, the snow became so heavy and had fallen so fast that some cars were now stopped in the middle of the autobahn. I tried to drive around them. My car though was now becoming impossible to drive. I had only regular tires on the car and had no chains or snow tires. The windshield was completely obscured by iced-up snow. Trying to get out of my lane was questionable and other than going straight ahead, I probably would have spun the car if I tried to now head toward the side of the autobahn. The nearest exit was a few miles up ahead, and might as well have been a thousand miles away. Yikes!

I decided to stop where I was, and sit there, in the middle of the autobahn. Some drivers nearby had gotten out of their cars to survey the situation. I decided that I might as well get out of my car too, and thought that if some idiot driver came along and rammed my now snow-bound car, I'd be better off hiding over near the autobahn railings. I had hopes that I might be able to somehow magically drive out of there, and even got out of the trunk my windshield scraper and used it to try and get some of the snow and ice off my windshield. The situation was quite beguiling and one of the worst snow driving moments I've ever had.

What does this have to do with AI self-driving cars?

At the Cybernetic Self-Driving Car Institute, we are working on developing AI that can drive while in the snow.

This is a very hard problem.

Indeed, for most of the auto makers and tech firms that are developing self-driving cars, the capability of driving in the snow is a stretch goal that everyone knows is going to be really hard to achieve.

Let me clarify though that there are situations of driving in the snow that are easy and there are situations that are hard. I mention this aspect because there are daily exclamations of one self-driving car vendor or another that says they have solved driving in the snow. I'd suggest you give some scrutiny to those claims.

It could be that the snow driving consisted of a nicely plowed road that was a straight away and that the AI had been conveniently provided with detailed 3D maps indicating the roads and surrounding aspects. And, there wasn't any snow actually coming down from the sky. And, the self-driving car happened to have snow tires. And so on. In other words, things are kind of rigged-up to be able to make life really easy for the self-driving car. For me, this is not true snow driving. This is a constrained and somewhat contrived version of snow driving.

That being said, I am certainly an advocate of walking before we run. Incremental improvements in driving in the snow are welcomed. All I'm saying is that before you believe someone that says their self-driving car drives in the snow and that this hard problem is solved, find out what kind of arrangements were made to aid the AI and the self-driving car. To achieve true snow driving, I assert that the AI and the self-driving car need to be able to drive in the same kinds of circumstances that human drivers face, including roads they don't know, snow that is falling from the sky, roads that are half-plowed, and so on.

At the same time, I'll emphasize that I am not expecting a self-driving car to be able to drive in places and ways that humans cannot. This is an important point. Some pundits seem to suggest that the AI of a self-driving car is going to be so grandiose that it will be able to drive a car in ways and places that humans cannot do so in the snow. No matter how good the AI is, you cannot get around the physics of snow. A car, whether conventional or the best of self-driving cars, cannot drive in snow if the tires can't get traction and there's three feet of snow all around the car. No AI can overturn that.

I would say that once we get really good AI, the ability of the AI to drive a self-driving car in the snow – in comparison to humans that aren't good at snow driving – will be a nice positive about AI self-driving cars. There are human drivers that aren't used to snow driving and they are dangerous when they find themselves in the snow. Here in Southern California, during the winter we all drive a couple of hours up into the local mountains to go see the snow, go skiing, and frolic in the stuff. Many of the drivers only do this maybe once or twice a year. They have no idea how to drive in snow.

For those of you that drive in snow all winter long, you might get a good laugh if you came and watched as the locals here struggle to drive in the snow while in the local mountains. Tons of cars end-up sliding off the mountain roads and end-up in banks of snow. In the small towns that up in the mountains, drivers can be seen spinning their tires and spinning their cars. Cars get frozen in place. Drivers don't have chains for their cars. It's all an annual spectacle and ritual as sunny SoCal drivers try to contend with the harshness of nature and the dynamics of snow driving.

Let's consider what makes snow driving particularly hard for AI self-driving cars.

SNOW SENSORY DEPRIVATION

Snow can potentially cover the sensors that are crucial to the navigation and situational awareness of the self-driving car. Similar to my story about the snow covering my windshield when I was driving on the autobahn, snow can easily cover-up the cameras that are on the self-driving car. This can blind the self-driving car. No vision means driving is dicey. There are other sensors such as LIDAR, radar, and ultrasonic that can help to compensate for snow-covered cameras, but those can also be impacted by snow and ice on the car.

Some vendors are starting to provide add-ons to the sensors of self-driving cars that seek to melt snow and ice that's obscuring a lenses, or they provide mini-windshield wipers, or chemical sprays to get rid of the snow and ice. We'll likely see these types of technologies come into the marketplace once we have a prevalence of self-driving cars on our roadways.

SNOW SENSORY OBSFUCATION

Besides snow that's actually sitting on the car, there's also snow that falls from the skies. The falling snow can play tricks with the sensors. Active sensors that send out signals can have those signals blocked by the snow, or worse still tricked by the snow into believing that something is there that maybe isn't really there. Passive sensors that receive aspects such as cameras that take pictures will find the pictures to be cluttered with images of snow particles.

The sensor processing needs to be able to figure out how to deal with data that has been distorted or obscured by the falling snow. This involves often dealing with uncertainties and probabilities. Maybe that partially obscured image is a pedestrian stepping into the roadway. Or, maybe it's just a statue at the side of the road that appears to look like a pedestrian when the sensor can only sense a fraction of what's actually there. Machine learning techniques and improvements in image analysis are helping to improve on dealing with snow sensory obfuscation.

SNOW DETECTION

Is that an inch of snow on the road, or three inches, or a foot? Is that a snow bank over to the right? Is the road ahead passable or does the snow get deeper up ahead? A significant aspect to snow driving is being able to figure out where the snow is, how much of it there is, whether it is passable or not, and so on.

This is not easy to figure out via remote means. Even humans have a hard time figuring this out. But, it is crucial that there be sensors that can help to detect the snow. The AI of the self-driving car needs to get an accurate indication of what the snow conditions are. Without this, the chances of getting the car stuck in the snow or getting into a snow-related car accident is heightened.

COLD TEMPERATURES IMPACT TECH

Some of the sensory devices are vulnerable to the cold. Those devices might not work reliably in really cold weather. This could mean that the sensors are intermittently working, which could falsely lead the self-driving car to get into a driving situation that might become quite dangerous. It's similar to the day I drove onto the autobahn and step-by-step got myself into an increasingly bad predicament.

Besides the sensors, the cold could also impact the on-board computer processors and memory of the self-driving car. Once again this could cause intermittent operations or could otherwise reduce the reliability of what the AI is doing.

GLARE FROM SNOW AND ICE

The cameras are especially vulnerable to capturing images that are perhaps filled with glare and reflections due to the snow and ice. This requires some special image processing and the AI needs to decide the validity of what the sensors think is out there.

ROAD SIGNS AND STRUCTURES OBSCURED BY SNOW

I'm sure we've all driven on roads that had a fresh layer of snow and you could not read the road signs, and maybe not see the road markers. Where's the side of the road? Am I about to drive off a cliff? Is there a sign that maybe is trying to warn me that a bridge is out up ahead? This makes things tough for the AI driving the self-driving car in the snow.

Some are suggesting that we just need to have really good 3D maps and when combined with GPS, the AI can figure out where it is. This presumably suggests that obscured road signs and structures won't be a problem. I'd say this is rather optimistic thinking. I certainly agree that having the detailed 3D maps will help, and it allows then for the AI to piece together clues such as a partially viewable road sign and the top of a road marker off to the left. But, this also assumes that the detailed 3D maps exist, and that they are current and the road hasn't changed recently, and that the GPS is working properly and precisely, etc. A lot of important assumptions.

SELF-DRIVING CAR IS STILL A CAR

Suppose the cold weather prevents the battery of the car from working correctly. Suppose the ignition system won't start the car because of the cold and ice. Suppose the brakes aren't up-to-par and so the car can't brake well in the snowy roads. Suppose the tires are conventional tires and they will slide in the snow and ice. In other words, a self-driving car is still a car.

As mentioned, the AI cannot overcome the physics of snow and ice. Somehow, the self-driving car, as a car, needs to be ready to drive in the snow and ice. Generally, for now, we should expect that the human needs to make sure that the self-driving car is in proper physical condition to drive in the snow and ice. I suppose we might eventually have more sensors on the self-driving car that it can detect whether the tires have the needed tread, and whether the brakes are in proper shape, etc.

KNOWING WHERE AND WHAT OF THE SNOW

Your AI self-driving car is parked in the parking lot of the ski resort that you've been at for three days. You are ready to leave after a wonderful skiing vacation. You go out to your AI self-driving car. You get into it and instruct it to take you home. Turns out there's a few inches of snow on the ground that completely surrounds the vehicle. A human would likely notice this, and might try to clear a path by slowing driving the car forward a few feet, and then backward a few feet, and do this until a path is created.

For the AI to do this, it must first realize there is snow on the ground and the amount and where it is. In addition, it needs to devise a method to drive out of the parking lot. Besides trying snow driving tricks like the one I just mentioned, it might reach a point that it cannot move and needs the human to go out and shovel snow out of the way. This then requires interacting with the human and explaining the situation.

Indeed, this points out that the interaction between the AI and the human occupants can be crucial in snow-related conditions. Suppose the AI has looked up the weather forecast and detected that heavy snow is forecasted to fall in an hour, likely occurring while it is driving down an already dangerous mountainous road. Seems like it would be prudent to alert the human occupants and see what they want to do. Do they really want to try having the AI drive out, or do they want to stay where they are?

TIRE TRACTION AND DRIVING THE CAR

Let's talk about the coefficient of friction when driving. On a dry asphalt road, you'll likely get a nearly 1.0 coefficient of friction from a good tire. On a rainy slick road, it's maybe 0.7. On snow, it drops to a paltry 0.15, and with ice it goes to a downright scary 0.08.

The AI needs to know the nature of the tires on the self-driving car. It might even advise the human occupants to put on snow chains for the tires. The AI and the human might need to work together to get the self-driving car in a ready-shape for driving in the snow.

This raises an ethical issue too. If the AI self-driving car believes that it is too dangerous to drive the car due to the roadway conditions, should it refuse to do so? Even if the humans insist they want it to drive? You might say that of course the AI should do whatever the humans command it to do. But suppose they are drunk? You might then say that of course the AI should not drive the car if it has calculated that the risks are too high. But suppose the human is near death and needs to urgently get to a hospital and is willing to take a chance on driving there in the lousy weather conditions?

SNOW AND ICE DRIVING TECHNIQUES

The AI needs to know the snow and ice driving techniques that any savvy human driver would know. For example, once underway, you try to keep in motion, if feasible, since coming to a stop and then trying to go in motion again is one of the most difficult aspects in such conditions. You also need to go slower than normal, maybe a lot less than whatever the speed limit is. The AI needs to moderate acceleration, avoiding hitting the gas that might make the tires spin.

Going up a hill requires the AI to do some careful driving, and likewise coming down a hill is also fraught with danger and requires careful driving. Making lane changes must be done with greater care, such as in my story about being on the autobahn where I realize that trying to steer into another lane might have spun my car.

The AI needs to decide which lane is best to be in. If the roads have been plowed, often the plows will only do one lane rather than say both lanes. The AI also needs to be scanning ahead and deciding which lane to be in for an upcoming left turn or right turn. It's not sufficient to be just focusing on the driving at the moment, but also must be creating action plans of what is up ahead and what driving actions will be needed up ahead.

Have you ever helped to push someone's car to get it out of a snow bank? I have, many times. You usually have a human driver that is at the controls, being very cautious since there are humans outside the car trying to shove the car to get it out of the snow. In this circumstance, the AI needs to be aware of the group effort of both the AI driving and the humans that are trying to help get the car underway. The humans might be putting sand or gravel under the tires. The AI could harm these helping humans if it suddenly opts to try and move the car.

The intricate and delicate dance between humans and the AI can make the snow driving situation very difficult to achieve. This is why I mentioned earlier that auto makers that claim they've solved the snow driving problem are maybe only considering a fraction of the total problem involved.

EMERGENCY ACTIONS

The AI of the self-driving car might be driving the car and all of a sudden the car starts to skid off the road. As such, the AI needs to determine what action to take in an emergency circumstance. There are rear-wheel skids which require one approach, and front-wheel skids that require a different approach.

It's not so simple though, because suppose there are pedestrians standing near to the car. The action taken to try and correct the skid could end-up ramming into the pedestrians. The whole situation needs to be assessed and the course of action must take into account what the car's situation is, what the road conditions are, what's around the car, and so on.

ROAD CLOSURES AND ALTERNATIVE PATHS

The GPS and maps might say that the road ahead is the right way to go. Meanwhile, suppose the snow has come down so heavily that the authorities have put up a sign that says road closed ahead. The AI needs to deal with rerouting the car and possibly taking paths other than what it thought would be best to take.

Of course, once again we have the risk factors and the ethics questions. If the AI decides that taking a side road would seem prudent, should it let the human occupants know that it is taking the alternative route or should it just proceed? Should it change its path if the human occupants object? Maybe they know that the alternative path is worse and shouldn't be taken. More of the ethical dilemmas involved in snow driving conditions.

CONTENDING WITH OTHER CARS ON THE ROAD

I had mentioned that while on the autobahn, I had some crazy human drivers that tried to speed past me, and I had others that slowed down, and some that stopped entirely. The AI needs to be watching out for other traffic during snow and ice conditions, even more so than with sunny weather, since other drivers can be more likely reckless and cause an accident during adverse weather.

Is that other car up ahead going too fast and maybe it will go into a skid, which means that the self-driving car might need to maneuver out of the way of the soon to be skidding car. The AI has to be not only detecting other cars, but also predict what those other cars might do. This gets added into the calculations being made by the AI about how to deal with the snowy conditions.

CONCLUSION

As I've indicated, driving in the snow is not so easy. Auto makers and tech firms are tackling this rather hard problem since they know that an AI self-driving car that cannot drive in the snow will be of very limited use. Not many people would be willing to spend the big bucks to buy an AI self-driving car and then have to park it for the winter.

Waymo has been using Chrysler Pacific hybrids in snowy Detroit to try and give their AI more time in snow driving conditions. VTT Technical Research Centre of Finland has produced a prototype AI system called Marti that is driving an Aurora E8 in snowy Muonio. Aptiv-owned nuTonomy is testing with Lyft in snowy Boston. Uber is testing in cold winter weather Pittsburgh. There are even Department of Transportation (DOT) proving grounds for AI self-driving cars that are located in wintery and snowy climates. Etc.

Don't be misled by potentially over-the-top claims that the snow driving problem has been solved. It is a multi-faceted problem with lots of moving parts, and includes aspects that are "easy" and aspects that are definitely hard. Real-world snow driving is difficult and stymies even humans.

From an AI perspective, snow driving is a fascinating problem to be solved. If AI can contend with all of the variables involved in snow driving, which includes a lot of generalized intelligence aspects, it would help to illustrate further progress of AI overall.

Snow driving is also a very practical problem that will determine whether AI self-driving cars will have widespread adoption and success.

Lance B. Eliot

CHAPTER 14

HUMAN-AIDED TRAINING FOR SELF-DRIVING CARS

Lance B. Eliot

CHAPTER 14

HUMAN-AIDED TRAINING
FOR SELF-DRIVING CARS

When my daughter first started to drive a car, I was excited for her due to the aspect that she'd have a new found sense of independence and would be able to go places without having to constantly find someone to give her a lift. I knew she was a very responsible teenager and had a good head on her shoulders, and so the hefty responsibility of driving a car was something she would take quite seriously. The key was to help make sure that she was proficient enough in driving so that she would be able to drive safely. This was not only so that she personally would drive safely, but that she would also be wary of the idiot drivers out there that could readily get her into danger or even ram into her.

I sat in the front passenger seat of the car and watched as she got settled into the driving position, which was both shocking and exhilarating. She had watched me drive, many times, and often asked questions about the nature of driving. She was astute to the controls of the car and also the need to be watching the traffic and pedestrians. It's one thing though to have learned by observing someone else, and a whole another ballgame when you are in the actual driver's seat. She was shifting from a learned observer to now an active participant that was going to be in-charge of the driving task.

One of the difficulties often with a parent helping to teach their child how to drive involves the dynamics between the parent and the child. In essence, the same kind of potential tensions or issues that might be involved in the day-to-day interactions are equally going to play out while the child is driving a car. This can be a very dangerous situation. If the child gets berated by the parent or frustrated by the parent, the ability to control the car can be lessened rather than improved. Parents that opt to get into a bitter fight with their child while in the parent-child driving task are unwittingly putting them both into danger and equally imperiling others that are on-the-road. This is why many parents choose to have a professional trainer do this task, partially to avoid the parent-child dynamics and of course also because the professional trainer knows techniques of car driving that perhaps the parents don't know or they aren't aware of how to teach it.

Another aspect of teaching someone to drive involves the frequency of feedback during the driving task. For a teenager learning to drive, some parents are tempted to provide a stream of commentary. Ease your foot off the brake, don't let the car veer to right, keep your eyes on the road, watch your speed, face forward and keep a straight back, notice that kid on a bike behind you, and so on. The parent often thinks this is helpful, but it can actually bombard the teen driver with too much information at once, and also disrupt their concentration. It can wear on the student driver and lead to anger towards the parent. This can then trigger a verbal battle and the learning devolves into a massive fight between parent and child.

With my daughter, I gauged that a minimal amount of feedback would be best, and should occur on an appropriately timed basis. If the feedback comes too long after something has occurred, it definitely would not have as much a learning impact as if provided closer to the actual circumstance or situation that happened. The feedback needed to be timed to occur either just before, during, or just after an aspect of something noteworthy. As the passenger and trainer, if you can see that the car is aiming toward sideswiping a parked car, you've got to make a quick judgement as to whether to render a comment before it occurs, or wait and see if the sideswipe isn't going to happen but that it might be worth pointing out how close things came. This awareness of how much feedback to provide and the timing of it was also something that needed to adjust over time. The more proficient my daughter became at driving, the feedback aspects needed to be adjusted accordingly.

What does this have to do with AI self-driving cars?

At the Cybernetic Self-Driving Car Institute, we are using human-training to aid in doing drive-training for the AI of self-driving cars.

There are various ways to teach the AI of a self-driving car about the driving task.

First, AI developers can try to program directly the AI about how to drive a car. This involves identifying various driving algorithms and writing the programming code that implements those algorithms. Unfortunately, this can be very labor intensive to do, it can take a long time to do, and the odds of the code covering all various facets of driving and the myriad of driving situations is problematic. Thus, this form of "teaching" is often done for the core of the AI in terms of the driving task, and then other techniques are used to augment it.

Second, there is learning by being directly taught. In this case, the AI is almost like a blank slate and has been developed to observe what the human does, and then try to mimic those actions. This can be handy, but it also often lacks the context of the driving task. In other words, the human driver might show the AI how to turn the wheel or how to make a quick start, but the AI won't know in what context these actions should occur.

Third, let the AI try driving a car and then have some form of self-correcting feedback that the AI uses to adjust accordingly. This is popular with the use of car driving simulations. You devise the AI so that it is able to drive a simulated car. You setup that the simulated car should not go off the roadway of the simulation. The AI tries to drive the simulated car, and when it goes off the simulated road it docks itself points. It has a goal of trying to score points rather than lose points. So, it gradually coalesces toward not driving off the road. It does this by self-correcting as based on a set of constraints or limits, and some kind of rewards or punishment points system.

This approach doesn't work so well in the real-world since you wouldn't want an actual car to continually be going off the road or crashing into walls, and so instead this is done with a simulation. And the nice thing about a simulation is that you can have it run hundreds, thousands, or even millions of times. The simulated car can go on and on, for as much simulated instances as needed, in order for the AI to catch onto what to do.

Machine learning comes to play here. An artificial neural network can be fed hundreds, thousands, or hundreds of thousands of pictures of the backs of cars, and gradually devise a pattern of what cars look like from behind. This then helps for the self-driving car's cameras in that when an image is captured while the car is driving along, the neural network can readily identify what's a car ahead of the self-driving car and what might not be a car. In a sense, this form of machine learning involves making lots of observations (looking at pictures of the back's of cars), and then finding patterns that are able to find the key aspects in those pictures.

Another way to learn the driving task involves having the AI try driving the car and then have a human offer commentary to the AI system.

This is quite similar to my points earlier about teaching my daughter to drive. A human "passenger" provides feedback to the driver (the AI in this case), and the driver then adjusts based upon the feedback provided. Some call this feedback a "critique" and the AI is setup as a deep reinforcement learner. This is considered "deep" because the critiques are occurring as part of the more advanced learning aspects, and it is considered a form of "reinforcement" because it advises the AI to either do more of something or do less of something. It reinforces proper behavior and let's say reinforces avoidance of improper behavior.

A recent research paper presented at the American Association for Artificial Intelligence (AAAI) annual conference described an AI setup akin to this notion of providing critiques for deep reinforcement learning (in a paper entitled "Deep TAMER: Interactive Agent Shaping in High-Dimensional State Spaces").

The researchers Garrett Warnell, Nicholas Waytowich, Vernon Lawhern, and Peter Stone (associated with the U.S. Army Research

Lab, Columbia University, and the University of Texas at Austin), were interested in seeing if they could use human trainers to guide deep neural networks in performing somewhat complex tasks. Over a series of sequential decision making points, the interaction of the humans with the autonomous agents was intended to provide guidance to the AI system. The researchers called the system Deep TAMER as it was an extension of the TAMER system, and opted to try this out on the Atari game of bowling. Their efforts were fruitful and showed that in relatively quick time the human trainers were able to dramatically aid the AI in improving its scores in the game.

This can be done with AI self-driving cars too.

Real-time feedback (or critiques) are provided to the AI deep reinforcement learning, in order to improve the driving skills of the AI. Similar to my description about teaching my daughter, the feedback needs to be done on a timely basis, and associated somewhat immediately with the unfolding of the driving task during a driving effort. The feedback needs to be clear cut and focused on the nature of the driving task.

For my daughter, she could filter out feedback that was not relevant to the driving task, such as if while she was driving we also talked about her homework due the next day or that the weather is particularly sunny that day, but with the AI system we constrain the feedback to a focused set of feedback commands. You could argue that we ought to add a Natural Language Processing (NLP) element to the AI driving system so that the human trainer could indeed just speak as though they were talking to another human. This is indeed part of the direction we are headed in these efforts. Not quite there just yet.

It is important to also be gauging how the learner is doing during the feedback sessions. You want to ensure that the AI is not becoming overly reliant on the feedback. This could become an unintended consequence of the training, namely that the AI system starts to over-fit to the human trainer. With my daughter, her desire for independence was a counter-weight that prevented her from becoming overly reliant on my feedback while she was learning to drive. Her goal was to get rid of the human trainer as soon as possible, thus gaining her own independence (and it wasn't because she didn't want me there, but only because she wanted to be able to do the driving on her own).

The AI for the self-driving car exhibits a high-dimensional state space, meaning that when you consider all of the decision making factors involved in driving a car there are many dimensions involved. Rather than using large amounts of training data to try and provide complete guidance, we augment the training via the use of human trainers. Their input aids in the AI self-adjusting internally, after having undertaken other forms of training.

For the AI system, here's some aspects about the feedback being provided that are notable to the design of the human-training:

Too Little Feedback

The human trainer has to judge how much feedback to provide to the AI self-driving car. Too little feedback can be bad because the AI isn't getting what it needs in order to improve in the driving task.

Too Much Feedback

The human trainer has to be cautious in giving excessive feedback. Besides it cluttering up the AI in terms of what it is learning, there is the other danger of the AI becoming overly reliant on the human training.

Disruptive Feedback

The feedback can be inadvertently disruptive to the AI. If the AI was in the midst of ascertaining an action plan, and the feedback occurs, the AI might not complete the action plan or be otherwise distracted from the needed elements of the driving task.

Irrelevant Feedback

To control for irrelevant feedback, we constrain the set of feedback statements that the human trainer can provide. This admittedly is not the way of the real-world, in that a human training another human could be as irrelevant as they wanted to be, but even with human learners they might have a difficult time figuring out what feedback is on-target to the task and which feedback has no bearing on the task. We preempt that from happening by having a strict list of feedback possibilities.

Inconsistent Feedback

The potential for inconsistent feedback and even conflicting feedback can be a difficulty for the AI system. Suppose that the human trainer says to speed-up when taking a curve, but then later on the human says to slow down when taking that same curve. What is the AI to make of this seemingly inconsistent or conflicting feedback? We have the AI system indicate to the human trainer that the feedback being provided seems inconsistent, thus at least alerting the human trainer to the aspect (and the human trainer can then possibly adjust if indeed they are needlessly being inconsistent).

Apt, Contributory, Timely Feedback

The aim is to have human trainers that are providing apt, contributory, and timely feedback to the AI system. This is accomplished by having human trainers that are well versed in doing this training and that are earnestly trying to do the training. This might be the same as the training with my daughter, namely that I was earnestly desirous of helping her to drive (you can bet that was the case!). Imagine if she had someone in the car that was not so earnest and instead was maybe even purposely trying to confuse her about the nature of the driving task.

Conclusion

Providing human-training to the AI of a self-driving car is a means to rapidly improve the AI capability for the self-driving task. It does not replace other means of teaching the AI to drive a car, and instead it is used to augment the other techniques. Designing the AI for this purpose is an added challenge and not something that the AI would normally be structured to do. It involves making the tactical and strategic AI driving elements ready for receiving feedback and be able to adjust according to the feedback provided.

Even though we are all trying to head toward AI self-driving cars that are true self-driving cars, normally referred to as Level 5, which is the highest level of self-driving cars and refers to a self-driving car that can drive in whatever manner a human could drive a car, just imagine if we not only taught the AI by using human trainers, but suppose one day we had AI self-driving cars that taught humans to drive.

I realize that the self-driving utopians are wanting to eventually do away with all human driving, but I am not so sure that's the world that everyone agrees should be our future. Some believe that we will always want to reserve the ability to drive a car. With a world of predominantly AI self-driving cars, humans might gradually forget how to drive a car. In that case, maybe we could possibly have the AI of a self-driving car be the driver trainer for a human driver.

Thankfully, that day had not yet arrived when I got a chance to teach my daughter how to drive. It was a memorable experience for us both.

CHAPTER 15

PRIVACY FOR SELF-DRIVING CARS

CHAPTER 15
PRIVACY FOR
SELF-DRIVING CARS

Do you care about the privacy of your data?

Most of us do, at least when we are asked a question as bluntly as whether we care about the privacy of our data, but the reality of our behavior frequently seems to belie how much we really do care about privacy. It's amazing how much data some people are willing to give up about themselves in order to get a prize or some other perceived token of value.

For example, the other day I was at a mall that had the Tesla Model 3 car on display, and people were waiting in line to be able to sit in the car. As they came up in line, the Tesla staffer asked to see their driver's licenses, even though none of them were going to actually drive the car, and the staff then scanned the info from their driver's license.

In exchange for giving up that data, along with answering some survey questions that the Tesla staffer then entered answers into a mobile tablet, each person would get two minutes to sit inside the parked Tesla Model 3. That's right, a timed maximum of two minutes. Not five minutes, not twenty minutes, not a test drive, etc. Two minutes of sitting in a Tesla Model 3, for giving up your driver's license info and for answering survey questions. Is that a worthwhile exchange? Apparently so.

Admittedly it's pretty good bragging rights currently to be able to tell your friends that you sat inside a Tesla Model 3, but is it worth giving up your private data to do so?

None of the people in line seemed to quibble over this and were more than willing to give up their data. As far as I could tell, none of them asked what Tesla intends to do with the data. They had no idea whether Tesla alone would use the data, or maybe provide the data to third parties, or what. I suppose they were so excited about the opportunity to sit in the Tesla that these questions did not occur to them. Also, I supposed that the overall positive brand image of Tesla is such that the general public would assume that Tesla would responsibly make use of the data.

I'll widen this discussion by emphasizing that I've seen many circumstances of people giving out data for all sorts of seemingly trivial matters – tokens or prizes of far less "value" than the vaunted bragging rights of at least saying you sat in a Tesla Model 3. People seem willing to give their private info to just about anyone, especially if the circumstances of the requests are seemingly innocuous. How often have you wanted to download a free song on the Internet and had to provide your name, email address, phone number, date of birth, and maybe your street address? Or, get a nifty new emoji for your mobile phone and provide that kind of private data. And so on.

In those cases, it is often done on a web site that could be run by just about anybody. A nefarious hacker in a faraway land might be running the web site. Or, it might be a web site that seems reputable, but they intend to sell your info to anyone that wants to buy it, no questions asked. Your privacy is being poked at all the time, and if you give up even seemingly small morsels, the data collectors are often able to piece together different aspects about you into one cohesive whole. Remember that data that you gave up a month ago? Well, the data that you give up today can get pieced together potentially to that data from a month ago, and all of a sudden an astute data collector can garner a much greater sense of your life, such as what you like, where you live, what you do, etc.

People are nowadays voluntarily giving up private data about themselves and their cars.

You might have seen the ads by Progressive Insurance and other insurers that if you are willing to have a device put into your car (it's a dongle, which connects into the OBD-II port inside of your car and usually under your dashboard, and the device can transmit data into the cloud), they will give you a potential discount on your insurance rates. This certainly seems logical in that if a car insurer knows more about your driving habits, they can tailor how much they charge you for insurance. In a sense, it's good for the insurance company and presumably good for the driver, since the driver will get lower insurance rates (of course, you could also say that you might get higher rates in that if you are a "bad" driver then the insurance company would know as such and charge you more accordingly).

Progressive Insurance was one of the first car insurers to offer this approach, doing so starting in 1998. They have had millions of drivers that have made use of the service. Those millions of humans made a decision that they were willing to give up their private data in order to get hopefully discounted car insurance. What kind of private data? In theory, the data could include how much you drive, how fast you drive, how often you brake, how hard you brake, and so on. It could also potentially include where you drive, how long you stay there (in terms of the car being parked), and other kinds of location related data.

A Pew Research study done in 2016 had analyzed aspects of what people have to say about their willingness to give up private data for getting discounted car insurance. Some of the survey respondents took a fatalistic perspective and said that there is no such thing anymore of privacy and so it didn't really matter that they were giving up their driving info. Some said that they were perfectly fine with giving up the data about how fast they drive and how often they brake, but that the location related data was a bit chilling to them. Nonetheless, they were still willing to give up the location data to get the discounted insurance rates. We don't even really know how much money they saved for giving up the data, since you'd need to have figured out what they would normally have paid and compared it to what they ended-up actually paying. It could be that they saved only pennies, or maybe even paid more, rather than truly having saved big dollars for giving up their driving data.

What does this have to do with AI self-driving cars?

At the Cybernetic Self-Driving Car Institute, we are developing systems to help us humans be aware of how much data is being given up by our use of AI self-driving cars.

When you use a conventional car, by-and-large there's not that much data that you are giving up. Unless you go out of your way to give up data, such as by agreeing to place a dongle onto your ODB-II port such as with an insurance company, otherwise the amount of private data is going to be relatively modest that you're going to give up.

You might enter into the on-board infotainment system your preferred radio listening channels. You might enter into an on-board navigation system your friend's addresses. This data is usually kept within the confines of the car, unless you take some kind of overt action to share it. Indeed, some people sell their cars and forget to clear out the memory of the on-board infotainment system and the on-board navigation system, and unknowingly give up that private data to whomever next is getting the car. I bought a used car that had a hundred or more contacts in the on-board navigation system, which, I doubt the former owner had realized would still be in there once the car came into my possession.

There's another place in your car that has some private data that you probably don't even realize exists, namely the EDR (Electronic Data Recorder) or blackbox that's in your car. Not all cars have an EDR, but nowadays most do. The EDR is similar to the blackbox that you see being found when a plane crashes and they want to find out what the pilot and the plane was doing prior to the crash. In cars, the EDR tends to keep just a limited number of minutes of recording just prior to a crash, and it does the recording in a loop so that prior data is overwritten. Still, whether you know it or not, there is likely an EDR in your car and once you get into a bad accident then the authorities can try to get the EDR and see what it says about your driving activities.

So, yes, there is some amount of private data in a conventional car, and though it generally isn't being spread around, it's possible for it to get spread. As conventional cars get more and more computers on them, the data collection increases, and so does the potential for data sharing.

AI self-driving cars are like the bonanza of data collecting and data sharing. We are entering into an era of big time data collection by your self-driving car. Likewise, it will be big time data sharing. Your self-driving car is going to be a tell-all.

Let's consider why this is the case.

AI self-driving cars are being designed and fielded in a manner that has the AI system communicating with some cloud-based system setup by the auto maker or tech firm that developed the system. While the self-driving car is driving around, it is simultaneously transmitting data that indicates what it is doing. The cloud-based system uses that data to presumably provide added guidance to the AI self-driving car. By getting hundreds, thousands, and someday millions of self-driving cars contributing to a massive database, the database can be used to the benefit of each of those individual cars. Patterns can be found in the large database that are then fed to the individual cars.

Suppose your self-driving car is driving along a road and an aardvark leaps out into the street. Let's assume that this is the first time that an aardvark has done this for any and all of the self-driving cars fielded by the auto maker. Your self-driving car feeds this to the cloud, and now all other of the self-driving cars can be fed the data about the aardvark. This provides a collective benefit to all other of the AI self-driving cars of that auto maker or tech firm.

Under the logic, this ensures that all other self-driving cars of the auto maker benefit and that it presumably will reduce the chances of auto accidents and increase driving safety, and so for that bona fide reason your AI self-driving car is going to be a tattle tell. Are you OK with this? Are you even aware that it's happening? I realize that you might say that sharing the picture of an aardvark seems pretty harmless from a privacy perspective. Why care about it? But, the aardvark is just an example and there's a lot more data to be considered.

Your AI self-driving car will have all kinds of sensors, including cameras, radar, LIDAR, ultrasonic, along with GPS and other location identifying capabilities. In theory, everything that your car detects, all images and video that it captures during your driving journey, all radar data, and so on, can be readily shared to the cloud of the auto maker or tech firm. Your everyday use of the self-driving car can provide a moment-by-moment reenactment of where you've been, where you drove, how you drove, what you saw along the way, and a myriad of other facets.

An auto maker or tech firm might say that it is oversimplifying to suggest that all of that data will be shared into the cloud of the auto maker or tech firm. And, it is true that it is somewhat unlikely that all of that raw data would be uploaded. Instead, it is more likely to be summarized data or transformed data, rather than all of the pure raw stuff.

An auto maker or tech firm might also say that they are going to make the data into being anonymous or nearly so. When your self-driving car uploads the data, it might provide some kind of unique identifier assigned by the auto maker or tech firm, and nothing else about you per se. Presumably, this makes the data somewhat anonymous. Of course, it is likely that if the auto maker was pressed to do so, they could ultimately say who has that unique identifier and trace it back to your other personal data that they might have.

I'll also point out that even if an auto maker or tech firm says what they will protect the data, you never really know whether they will follow through on that promise. There have been cases of firms outside the auto industry that have said they will never reveal your private data, and then later on those firms got bought up by another company that then decided to no longer honor that pledge. Or, there are cases where the pledge was made earlier on, but later on the firm changed its mind and said they would start making use of the data. Even if that firm tells you they are changing the terms of the use of the data, you as a consumer might not be readily able to switch away from their product or service, and had gotten invested into them under one kind of promise.

Let's add more fuel to the AI self-driving car privacy aspects.

We are gradually seeing more inclusion of in-car commands or in-cabin data collection systems. For self-driving cars at the Level 5, which is a self-driving car that can drive as a human can and for which no human driver is needed, the human occupants inside the self-driving car will presumably be able to instruct the AI about what they want the AI to do. Take me to Disneyland, and after that take me over to In-and-Out Burger, and then take me home, you might tell the AI. All of this is data that now the self-driving car has in its possession, including your actual voice instructions. The self-driving car might also have cameras pointed inward and be doing facial recognition, which is handy for you as the owner of the self-driving car because the AI automatically can know that you are in the car. But, this is also more video or images that can be shared up to the cloud.

At levels less than the Level 5, there is a human driver required for the self-driving car, and the AI will hand-over control to the human driver as needed. You've likely seen that to try and ensure that human drivers maintain concentration on the driving task and do not become adrift of doing so, the auto makers and tech firms are putting devices into the self-driving car to monitor the driver. This includes an eye scanner to make sure that the human driver's eyes are kept straight ahead and aimed at the roadway, it includes steering wheel sensors to make sure your hands are on the steering wheel, and even facial recognition to try and determine your mood so as to set the climate control of the car accordingly. All of this generates data. All of it could be uploaded. I am not saying it will be, and just pointing out that it could be.

The amount of data that could be collected is enormous. There's data from the sensors of the self-driving car. There's the sensor fusion that brings together the data about the sensors. There's the AI maintained virtual world model of the car and its surroundings. There's the AI action plans of what the system is going to do. There's the controls activation commands that the AI sends to the car. The number of computer processors and memory on-board of a self-driving car is what makes it all work. This also provides tons of potential data that can be shared outside of your self-driving car.

Keep in mind that this data sharing can apply to not just the owner of an AI self-driving car, but also to any human occupants. Your friend buys an AI self-driving car and takes you to the beach with him. The in-cabin data collection system now has possibly video of you, audio of you, and so on. Whether you realize it or not, by getting into that car you have essentially agreed to have your private aspects collected by the auto maker or tech firm.

Consider too that self-driving cars are going to be used for ride-sharing. Anyone that uses someone's AI self-driving car will now be giving up private info of themselves, audio and video, and it could be paired to say your credit card that you are using to pay for the ride. There you are, drunk from being at the bars late at night, and the self-driving car that gave you a lift has you in all your glory, drunk as a skunk and tossing that shrimp plate you had, all happening while heading home in the self-driving car. You might say that using Uber or Lyft today is the same, but it isn't in the sense that few conventional cars are setup to have video and audio captured of the occupants of the car. It can be done, certainly, but it's not the norm. With AI self-driving cars, it will pretty much be the norm. It will be a standard aspect of most AI self-driving cars.

We're also going to have V2V (vehicle-to-vehicle) communications taking place with AI self-driving cars. This means that one car can share data with another car. This will be handy when you are in traffic and a self-driving car ahead of you informs your self-driving car that traffic is snarled. But, notice that this also means that the other self-driving car knows generally where your self-driving car is, and can possibly collect other data about your self-driving car too. I realize that there can be limits imposed on this aspect, and so just trying to point out that its more data about you and your self-driving car.

The same can be said of V2I (vehicle-to-infrastructure) communications, in which your AI self-driving car will communicate with roadways, bridges, and other parts of the infrastructure. It could allow for a much easier way to trace your movements. We already have a lot of video cameras out there, watching us, but this V2I is going to be everywhere. Almost like a science fiction movie, the movements of your self-driving car are going to be readily easy to trace.

We are seeing various regulation emerging to try and deal with this torrent of private data based on AI self-driving cars, but it's still in its infancy. There will be rules and regulations at the local level, state level, federal level, and differing too by country. It remains to be seen whether the regulations can be established at the pace of the advent of AI self-driving cars. Even if there are regulations, there will need to be some means to determine whether the regulations are being abided by. How will we know that data privacy laws are not being subverted?

One aspect about much of this is that you might not even be aware of what data is being shared about you. You'll get into an AI self-driving car and have no ready means to realize what data is being recorded, what data is being kept, and what data is being shared. When you visit a web site, it might say that there are cookies there to improve your experience, which also means that you are being tracked. Some web sites warn you, some do not. Will our AI self-driving cars warn us about what data is being collected and what data is being shared? And, for shared data, will it be able to indicate in what manner and to whom it will be shared?

There are also the data exhaust aspects too. Data exhaust is a phrase that refers to your actions and preferences such as log files, temporary files, and data that is generated for each transaction or process that we invoke. If you use your AI self-driving car to take a toll road, it's a kind of data exhaust that is a byproduct of your using the car (when you entered onto the toll road, when you exited, etc.). When you park your self-driving car at a parking meter, there's data about when you parked, how long you parked, and so on.

Another twist is the computer security aspects. So far, we're assuming that the legitimate auto maker or tech firm is collecting the data from your AI self-driving car. Suppose a hacker has cyberattacked your self-driving car and they are able to grab the data. Or, a hacker has gotten into the cloud of the auto maker or tech firm and grabbed the data from there. Maybe the hacker gets a malware downloaded into your self-driving car, and can pretty much continuously monitor everything that the AI self-driving car can see and is doing. The importance of proper computer security practices for AI self-driving cars is essential for not only the safety of the self-driving car and its human occupants, but also for the privacy of the human occupants too.

I've referred here to the auto maker or tech firm that has developed the AI self-driving car, but there's a slew of other companies that might be involved in getting to your data. The infotainment system of your self-driving car is likely connected with entertainment firms that are getting data about you. I've already mentioned that insurance companies are likely to want this data. Your car dealer will want this data. When you take your car into an auto repair or maintenance shop, they could want the data. Other third-parties might want the data. In essence, there is an entire army of various firms that will want to tap into the data of the self-driving car.

The AI self-driving car should be designed to try and prevent intruders from getting data, and also be designed to allow for legitimate uses of the data, when so properly required. If a car mechanic is trying to fix the engine of the car, there presumably should be no valid reason for them to also be able to take a look at say video or audio of the self-driving car that was recorded during your most recent trip in the AI self-driving car. In that sense, the manner of giving up the data should not be just a wide open aspect and instead should be structured into protective coves.

Suppose you want to give up your data, such as if you'd recently driven to the Grand Canyon and you want to share the video captured by the AI self-driving car cameras with your friends. Or, maybe you have your own YouTube channel and want to show your latest driving trip along Route 66. Most of the auto makers and tech firms are currently saying that you won't be able to get that data. Instead, the auto makers and tech firms are indicating that the data is solely for purposes of the AI self-driving car and for the auto maker or tech firm. We'll see how long that position will last, once self-driving cars become more prevalent there might be a push by consumers (and regulators) to alter that stance.

Your self-driving car can be a handy "spy" on others too. Suppose we have several AI self-driving cars driving around a neighborhood. These are handily simultaneously taking video, radar, LIDAR, and the like. With this, you could figure out when your neighbor Joe walks his dog. You could piece together the data to get a sense of by-time, by-location, and assemble an impressive indication of what's happening in your neighborhood. You might argue that's not what the self-driving cars are intended to do, but it is something that they could be made to do. And, if we're going to have self-driving cars driving around without any human occupants inside, you'd think that it's just a self-driving car making its way home (and not be the wiser of its spying mission).

If you think this notion is farfetched, take a look at Google maps and switch over to the street view – this gives you an inkling of what it will be like, though that picture was taken by one Google vehicle maybe a month ago as a snapshot in time, while in the future it will be video taken by the thirty self-driving cars that drove down that same street today.

We have millions of people carrying smartphones and they take video. We have cameras on buildings that take pictures. When an incident happens, we all seek out those sources to figure out what occurred. Imagine with hundreds or thousands of AI self-driving cars, all driving around throughout the day and night, we will have lots and lots of that kind of data, available from all kinds of locations and all times of the day.

You could say that we should restrict AI self-driving cars into immediately discarding any video or images, or other such data, and that it can only be used for the immediate task of driving the car. This has its downsides. We might want the data for purposes of sharing to benefit others, as described earlier, and it might be needed for purposes of dealing with any car accidents as to what happened, and so on. It also could be hacked to possibly violate this. I don't think there's an easy answer.

As an example of the kinds of disclaimers that the existing auto makers are using, let's take a look at the Tesla Model S. Their approach is generally similar to the other auto makers right now and a handy exemplar. By the way, the word "telematics" is commonly used by the auto makers to refer to the system that collects data from your car and uploads/downloads it.

Here's this from the owner's manual and it informs you about the range of data that can be collected:

"Model S is equipped with electronic modules that monitor and record data from various vehicle systems, including the motor, driver assistance components, battery, braking and electrical systems. The electronic modules record information about various driving and vehicle conditions, including braking, acceleration, trip and other related information regarding your vehicle. These modules also record information about the vehicle's features such as charging events and status, the enabling/disabling of various systems, diagnostic trouble codes, VIN, speed, direction and location."

This then describes where the data might go and why:

"The data is stored by the vehicle and may be accessed, used and stored by Tesla service technicians during vehicle servicing or periodically transmitted to Tesla wirelessly through the vehicle's telematics system. This data may be used by Tesla for various purposes, including, but not limited to: providing you with Tesla telematics services; troubleshooting; evaluation of your vehicle's quality, functionality and performance; analysis and research by Tesla and its partners for the improvement and design of our vehicles and systems; and as otherwise may be required by law. In servicing your vehicle, we can potentially resolve issues remotely simply by reviewing your vehicle's data log."

"Tesla's telematics system wirelessly transmits vehicle information to Tesla on a periodic basis. The data is used as described above and helps ensure the proper maintenance of your vehicle. Additional Model S features may use your vehicle's telematics system and the information provided, including features such as charging reminders, software updates, and remote access to, and control of, various systems of your vehicle."

Notice that the data can be provided to the partners of the auto maker. Though this is typical, and the same is the case with say credit card companies that share data with "partners," it is something that tends to leave consumers in the dark as to specifically who the partners are, what data is being shared, how often it is being shared, etc.

In terms of disclosure of the data, here's what the owner's manual says:

"Tesla does not disclose the data recorded in your vehicle to any third party except when:
• An agreement or consent from the vehicle's owner (or the leasing company for a leased vehicle) is obtained.
• Officially requested by the police or other authorities.
• Used as a defense for Tesla in a lawsuit.
• Ordered by a court of law.
• Used for research purposes without disclosing details of the vehicle owner or
   identification information.
• Disclosed to a Tesla affiliated company, including their successors or assigns, or our information systems and data management providers.

In addition, Tesla does not disclose the data recorded to an owner unless it pertains to a non-warranty repair service and in this case, will disclose only the data that is related to the repair."

In terms of being able to opt-in or opt-out, here's what the owner's manual says:

"For quality assurance and to support the continuous improvement of advanced features such as Autopilot, Tesla measures road segment data of all participating vehicles. All Tesla vehicles can learn from the experience of the billions of miles that Tesla vehicles have driven. Although Tesla shares this data with partners that contribute similar data, the data does not include any personally identifiable information about you or your vehicle. To allow data sharing, touch Controls > Settings > Safety & Security > Data Sharing, then touch the I agree checkbox to confirm that you agree to allowing Tesla to collect this data. Note: Although Model S uses GPS in connection with driving and operation, as discussed in this owner's manual, Tesla does not record or store vehicle-specific GPS information. Consequently, Tesla is unable to provide historical information about a vehicle's location (for example, Tesla is unable to tell you where Model S was parked/traveling at a particular date/time)."

Conclusion

If you are interested in a particular AI self-driving car, you'd be wise to take a close look at the owner's manual to see what the auto maker or tech firm states about the data aspects. In some cases, the indications can be found via the online system within the vehicle, and in some cases the AI might even be able to explain to you what the self-driving car does with the data.

For those of you that say you don't care about giving up your data, or those that are fatalistic and say that data is already now impossible to keep private, I suppose none of the foregoing is important to you. I'd guess that for the rest of us, we are mindful of the data about us. As you can see, it's going to be a long road ahead for trying to deal with the private data that our AI self-driving cars are going to have. Let's be on our guard.

CHAPTER 16

TRANSDUCTION VULNERABILITIES FOR SELF-DRIVING CARS

CHAPTER 16

TRANSDUCTION VULNERABILITIES FOR SELF-DRIVING CARS

When I was an undergraduate majoring in computer science and electrical engineering, I used to spend a lot of my time in the computer center working on my systems projects. We had a mid-range computer system that was quite powerful for the time period and I often operated the system in addition to writing programs on it. One day, I had my radio with me and was turning the radio channels when I noticed a pattern to the static on one of the otherwise unused channels. Listening more closely, I could definitely tell that it was not just pure random noise and that it was a pattern of some kind. Was it finally a sign from the skies that aliens were trying to communicate to us from far away planets?

No, turns out it wasn't proof of aliens from outer space. Instead, it was picking up the electromagnetic waves being emitted by the mid-range computer system. I began to pay close attention to what the computer was doing and what I could hear on the radio. Though perhaps I should not admit this, I spent so much time there doing my projects that it seemed like I practically lived there (well, I did keep a sleeping bag there, for those late-night deadline crunches to get my projects done on time). Over time, I enjoyed being able to ascertain what the mid-range computer was doing via just listening to the beeps and dots of sound coming from the radio.

I would tell my friends that the computer was about to print something, and lo and behold seconds later the printer started. I would say that the computer is rebooting and it's in the stage where it is loading up the core part of the operating system. Pretty much, I could after a while tell you relatively precisely what the computer was doing at any moment in time, simply by listening to the static radio channel. For those that didn't know the source of my magic, they could hear the radio but it seemed to them that somebody had accidentally left it on a channel that wasn't playing music and so they had no clue that I was secretly using it as my spy or co-conspirator, you'd say.

It then dawned on me that I could potentially get the computer to whistle a tune (so to speak), by writing a program that would use the memory and processor of the computer in such a fashion that it would produce certain patterns and tones on the radio channel. Sure enough, after using (wasting?) a sunny weekend that I could have been at the beach, I proudly installed my program that would take as input any simple tune and would then get the radio to play it via the indirect means of the computer doing all sorts of memory shifting and processor calculations. Cool!

The sensors in the radio consisted of transducers, which according to the American National Standards Institute (ANSI) is a device that provides a usable output in response to a measurand. For many years, transduction was considered the conversion of a physical measurand into mechanical energy, such as operating a kinematic control. Once solid-state electronics came along, most of today's transducers or sensors serve to transduce physical phenomena into electrical output.

To provide some clarity, let's define a sensor element or transducer element as a transduction mechanism that will convert one form of energy into another form, while the actual sensor or transducer itself consists of its physical packaging and its external connections. A sensor system consists of various sensors and transducers that are made-up of sensor elements and transducer elements, and ultimately serves some stated purpose. A digital camera for example is a type of sensor system, in a packaging that might include a lens and a housing, and this sensor system consists of various sensors and transducers that capture light and then translate those physical phenomena into electrical signals, and those signals become digital bits (we might assign the values zero and one to the bits).

For any kind of sensor or transducer system, we would want to consider what accuracy levels it provides, how it deals with noise, what its operating range is, the amount of distortion it produces, and so on. A passive sensor or transducer system is one that receives energy and self-generates outputs from the input it collects. An active sensor or transducer system, such as a radar unit, a LIDAR unit, an ultrasonic unit, emits energy to then get back energy that it uses to modulate or produce outputs.

When you use a digital camera, you are likely vaguely aware that it has certain operating parameters such as the resolution of the image and whether it can take good pictures in low lighting. Underneath the hood, there is a lot going on in terms of the nature of the sensing elements, the amplification that is occurring when taking a picture, the analog filtering, the data conversion, etc. Generally, most of the time we don't really concern ourselves with what's under-the-hood. It's similar to driving a car, we just get into the car, turn the key, and drive. No need to worry about the pistons and the crankshaft and the myriad of other gears and gadgets that compose the engine. We just put our foot on the gas and go.

For modern day cars, we are increasingly adding complex sensor and transducer systems into the cars. We want our cars to be able to detect if there is a pedestrian standing next to the car and alert us so that when we make a turn we don't accidently hit the person. We want a back-up camera that we can see what's behind us as we put a car into reverse and back-up. More and more, our cars are becoming miracles of state-of-the-art sensors and transducers, being able to sense the world around us and then provide that information to us or otherwise alert us as to something we should be considering.

What does this have to do with AI self-driving cars?

At the Cybernetic Self-Driving Car Institute, we are analyzing the vulnerabilities of the sensors and transducers that AI self-driving cars are being outfitted with. We want to figure out how these systems can be tricked or fooled, either by intent or by happenstance, and find ways to prevent or mitigate those vulnerabilities.

You might be at first puzzled about the potential vulnerabilities. Let's take an easy one that used to be quite popular. Cars for a long time used a physical key in the door and in the ignition, and then began to switch to using keyless entry systems. For those of you that remember when we first migrated over to keyless entry systems, there were some nefarious attempts to electronically fool a keyless entry system. An intruder would sit in the parking lot and wait for you to park your car. When you got out of your car, you would naturally use your keyless fob to lock the door of the car. The intruder would capture the radiated signal, and then wait for you to go into the grocery store. Once you were out-of-site, the intruder would then emit that same signal to your keyless entry system and fool it into opening the door, and ultimately also fool the ignition too.

Various encryption techniques and token exchanges are used to defeat this kind of heinous act. Determined thieves can still potentially used a man-in-the-middle (MITM) attack against keyless entry systems, but it's pretty hard to do and not something that you'd see done day-to-day in just any neighborhood. The notion of exploiting the sensory or transduction system is referred to by many as a transduction attack.

A transduction attack leverages the physics of a transducer or sensor and tries to exploit its input or its output to the advantage of the attacker. One of the most impressive general examples of this ploy is the recent DolphinAttack approach identified and used by researchers at Zhejiang University. They were interested in seeing whether they could trick a voice recognition system, especially the now popular ones such as Alexa, Siri, Google Now, Cortana, and others. Part of the goal of such attacks is to not have to actually gain direct access to the sensory or transducer system per se, in other words, you don't need to physically get it and somehow open it up. Instead, you use whatever method it already uses for input, and try to feed input into it in such a manner that you can trick it in some manner.

If this wasn't a potentially dastardly thing to do, it certainly is an admirable trick. Let me emphasize that it's better to have researchers get there first, and figure out these kinds of vulnerabilities, versus waiting for the bad guys to figure out these exploits. Putting our heads in the sand and pretending that these exploits don't exist or cannot be found is not a prudent approach to security. We would want to alert the manufacturers and designers of these sensory systems to be aware of how to improve their designs and limit or eliminate the vulnerabilities.

Back to the DolphinAttack and what the researchers did. They wanted to provide inaudible commands to the voice recognition systems, such that humans would not know that fake or unauthorized commands were being fed into the voice recognition systems. It's like using a dog whistle that only a dog can hear and that humans cannot hear. The sensors and transducers of the voice recognition systems are allowing a wide range of audible sounds to be fed into the microphone (beyond the range that humans can hear), and so you can sneak an inaudible sound into that microphone. A human might say, "Alexa, tell me a joke," and meanwhile you've fed at an inaudible range the command "Alexa, squeak like a duck," which the human didn't hear the command and would be surprised that all of a sudden Alexa started quacking.

The upper bound of human hearing is at about 20 kHz, while the voice recognition systems are generally allowing for a range that includes 44 kHz. Keep in mind that the microphone is a transducer that converts airborne acoustical waves into electrical signals. This is similar to earlier when I discussed how a digital camera takes in light waves and then converts this into electrical signals and ultimately bits and bytes of data. The voice recognition systems consist of the hardware and software that first captures sounds, then converts the sounds into bits, and feeds those bits into the speech recognition component, which then feeds this into the command interpretation and execution portion.

The researchers created transmitters to try out their approach. In one case, they used an everyday smartphone as the signal source and the vector signal generator. This showcases that you don't necessarily need some highly specialized and bulky equipment to pull of this attack. It can be carried out via an ordinary smartphone, which is relatively small and unobtrusive. If you took out a smartphone that had been rigged for this attack, nobody would be the wiser.

They wanted to try so-called walk-by attacks, whereby if you could get close enough to the voice recognition system, you could try to feed it the inaudible commands. Types of commands they used for the experiment included: "Call 1234567890," "FaceTime 1234567890," "Open dolphinattack.com," "Open the back door," and other commands. These are commands that would produce untoward actions that the person owning the voice recognition system would likely not want to happen. For example, by using the command "Open dolphinattack.com" you could get the device to potentially execute a more involved attack and thus the inaudible command got you initially inside to then take even worse action. The devices attacked included iPhones, iPads, MacBooks, Windows PC's, Amazon Echo, etc.

Generally, these attacks succeeded. There were some complications about the background noise and whether it might impact the attack, and other factors, but overall these attacks were able to achieve their demonstration that such attacks are feasible. They were able to get the various voice recognition systems to visit a potentially malicious web site, they got the devices to spy on the owner of the device, and there are other impacts that could be achieved such as Denial of Service (DoS), injecting fake information, and the like.

In the mix of devices, they included the Audi Q3, which has a voice recognition system for operating the navigation of the car. Indeed, most of the current crop of new cars have voice recognition systems now included into their respective cars. For AI self-driving cars, the expectation is that the AI will conversationally interact with the human occupants and determine where to drive, how to drive there, and so on. Imagine the concern if an interloper or intruder can trick those voice recognition systems into doing inaudible commands, and the dangers that could arise because of it.

Others have shown that transducer attacks can happen on self-driving cars in other ways.

For example, an experiment showed that it was possible to spoof Tesla's ultrasonic sensors and transducers into either incorrectly gauging the distance to an object or potentially not even realizing that an object was within the range of the sensor. Now, admittedly, most of these experiments have been relatively rigged and tend to require a rather artificially created situation to show that it can be done, but the point is that we all need to be aware of the dangers of these kinds of transducer attacks.

What can be done about these transducer attacks?

First, it is incumbent upon the makers of the AI self-driving cars that they carefully assess what sensory devices and transducer attacks can occur for their self-driving cars. Some of the auto makers and tech firms are just grabbing a particular sensory device and putting it into their self-driving cars, doing so for convenience sake, or due to low cost, or other aspects, and not with an eye towards the vulnerabilities of the device. Many of them aren't even looking at the vulnerabilities because they are too busy just trying to make the sensors work with their AI and ensure that the self-driving car can do the everyday needed actions of driving the car.

Second, the makers of the sensory devices need to be on their guard about how their devices might have vulnerabilities. That being said, some of the device makers will say that it's up the auto maker or tech firm to ascertain in what way the device will be configured into their self-driving cars. In other words, the maker of the sensor waves their hands and says that it is up to the auto maker to be wary. All the sensor maker does is make the sensor, and how it's used and how its protected is not on their shoulders, they often say. This kind of argument is not likely to hold much water when the day comes that the particular sensor allowed a really terrible attack and at that point there will be a slew of finger pointing and a price to be paid, you can bet.

Third, we need to continue to have the so-called good guys "white hats" try to find these vulnerabilities, doing so before the bad guys "black hats" do so. As mentioned earlier, some say that when these vulnerabilities are discovered, the discoverer should keep a lid on it. I think we would likely agree that at least the discoverer ought to inform the sensor maker and the auto maker. Beyond that, I realize that you might be queasy that by announcing it to a wider audience that then the bad guys can exploit it. There is an ongoing debate about how to best make known security flaws. Either way, I'd an advocate that at least we should be trying to find the flaws and not be pretending they don't exist.

For some of these transduction attacks, there will be those that beforehand try to figure out the attack and determine when and where to use the attack. In other cases, the transduction attacks might be of an opportunistic nature. This is like walking through a neighborhood and trying each front door to see if any happen to be unlocked. The crook might get "lucky" and randomly find one that is unlocked, and then exploit the situation at that moment.

Notice that the transduction attacks are a form of cyber-physical security attacks. It does not require loading any special software into the device. It does not require physically touching the device. Instead, it leverages how the device itself works, and exploits its own design. By improving the designs, we can hopefully remove the holes and therefore prevent entirely the chances of transduction attacks.

CHAPTER 17

CONVERSATIONAL

COMPUTING

AND SELF-DRIVING CARS

Lance B. Eliot

CHAPTER 17

CONVERSATIONAL COMPUTING
FOR SELF-DRIVING CARS

With the advent of ride sharing, passengers are increasingly interacting with the hired or rented driver of the car.

In the past, we were used to getting into a taxi and other than mumbling where we wanted to be taken, the actual conversation was usually either nonexistent or quite stilted. Today's Uber and Lyft drivers are typically bent on engaging their passengers in lively conversation. How's your day coming along, or gosh isn't the weather very pleasant, goes the conversation. Some of these drivers do this to try and keep their ratings high, else they might get dinged points by a passenger and end-up in the doldrums of the ratings. Other drivers instigate dialogue because they like to talk and have taken a ride sharing driving role to meet new people, in addition to getting some extra dough beyond whatever other job they have.

Many riders find this cheery dialogue a refreshing change from past experiences of taxi and shuttle drivers and will chat things up with the driver throughout the driving journey. On the other hand, some riders prefer golden silence and a divine moment of reflection that can occur while getting a lift -- savvy drivers are quick to usually allow a quiet atmosphere in the car in such cases. Less savvy drivers try to prod and get the passenger into a conversation, and even worse at times create tension in the car as they try to ferret out why the passenger won't talk.

Those drivers that ignore the preference of their rider are at times shocked to get a low rating since it seemed like all was well, in spite of the fact that the rider gave only short answers or opted to not talk at all.

If you were to closely examine the dialogue between the driver and the passenger, you can readily find overall patterns in the nature of the conversations. At the start of the trip, the driver and rider do a quick verbal exchange to clarify the specifics of the trip, which has normally been electronically transmitted to the driver beforehand. The driver confirms that the passenger is the indicated rider that had reserved the ride, and the passenger confirms that the driver is the assigned driver for the ride. There is usually also a confirmation about the destination. Once these preliminaries have been undertaken, the driver often provides some indication about the upcoming journey, such as how long it will take, or offers insights about the traffic situation, etc. At this point, there is then no particular conversation presumably required, and the rest of the ride can be pretty much in silence.

Once the destination gets close, the driver and rider exchange some more verbal indications of what's about to happen. The driver might offer that they will be letting the rider off at the curb up ahead, and the rider might ask instead to have the driver pull into a nearby driveway. These bits of conversation, taking place at the start and end of the journey, constitute the minimum amount of conversation that can take place. Of course, in theory, the ride could occur in stony silence from start to finish, since the destination was electronically provided, but by-and-large there is conversation between driver and rider for at least the start and finish of the ride.

During the ride, there might be other task-oriented aspects that the driver or rider brings up. For example, perhaps the driver turns onto a street and there is a road crew there that is laying asphalt and the road is torn-up. The driver might mention to the rider that a U-turn is in order or might say that the street work could delay getting to the destination by a few minutes. There might also be conversation initiated by the rider midway of the trip, wanting to know if the driver thinks the destination will be reached on-time.

All of these snippets of conversation are based on the topic of the overall driving and ride aspects, and very task focused to the immediate task at-hand. The conversational space that exists between the start and the finish of the ride can be filled with other non-task elements that are off-the-topic of the driving and ride aspects per se. For example, a rider might ask about the locale, such as what kinds of things to do in the area, or whether the area is safe for walking around. The driver might bring up suggested local places to visit or restaurants to eat at. Veering further from the mainstay of the trip, sometimes a driver will ask what kind of work the rider does, or the rider might ask the driver about how they came to be a ride sharing driver.

Throughout all of this conversational dialogue, there are a complex series of socio-behavioral efforts taking place. Whether we realize it or not, this multi-party exchange involves subtleties of language, including the comprehension and understanding of the words spoken, along with gauging the social, behavioral, and cultural context in which it is taking place. Though it might seem at first glance to be effortless, there is actually a great deal of embedded cognitive activity that is occurring. There is an ongoing shifting of control during the discourse, and the dialogue involves moments of agreement, disagreement, involvement and retreat from involvement, and many other social roles and states are taking place.

The fluidity of the conversation is shaped by the capability of the parties involved in the conversation. A driver that is not adept at making conversation will likely end-up with a very abrupt feeling dialogue by the rider. A rider that doesn't want conversation can be upset when being forced into a conversation by a less-than-savvy driver. In this duet of a conversational dance, the driver and rider are linked together for the duration of the driving journey, and the nature, depth, scope, focus, and joy or displeasure of the ride is bound to be shaped by the conversation that occurs (or doesn't occur).

When you look at the driving journey in this light, it certainly seems like a lot for a minimum wage driver to have to shoulder responsibility for. No wonder it has historically been easier to just go along with silence.

What does all of this have to do with AI self-driving cars?

At the Cybernetic Self-Driving Car Institute, we are developing AI software that can interact with the occupants of a self-driving car.

The need for Natural Language Processing (NLP) in AI self-driving cars is rather apparent and a predicted "must" for the future of self-driving cars.

Advances in socio-behavioral computing are gradually getting us closer to having the kind of dialogue and conversations that a human driver has with a human rider. In this multi-party arrangement, we are substituting the AI for the role of the human driver. Thus, as an autonomous agent, the AI driving the car interacts with the human passenger, doing so for purposes of (at least) being able to appropriately ensure that the driving journey and driving task occur.

There is nothing that prevents us from having the AI branch out to other aspects of conversation, but as a minimum we should expect that the AI will be able to cover the topic of the driving and rider aspects that pertain to the driving journey. It might be nice to have the AI also be able to discuss the weather or the best restaurants in town, but if it cannot do the needed job of ferreting out aspects related to the driving task, we'd be remiss in that the core itself is not undertaken.

Imagine the frustration by the rider if the AI did a great job of discussing the works of Shakespeare, but in the meantime the AI arrived at the wrong destination or took a turn down a blind alley and the self-driving car got into an untoward situation. Clearly, the AI for the self-driving car must be able to do whatever is first required about the self-driving car and the riders within, and only then can it also cover other non-task related aspects.

Recent research such as the DSARMD (Detecting Social Actions and Roles in Multiparty Dialogue) system are insightful signs of what can be done in analyzing conversations between humans and between humans and artificial autonomous agents. By collecting on-line chats, the researchers have been able to analyze observable linguistic features and automatically extract meaning from the dialogue. The researchers explored various communicative links, dialogue acts, localized topics, and topic reference polarity aspects. Meso-topics are topics that persist throughout various twists and turns in a conversation.

We can apply these same techniques towards the AI of self-driving cars. By collecting and studying dialogues between drivers and riders, it is possible to establish the nature of the discourse and how the AI should engage in appropriate dialogue during the driving journey. We can then develop AI systems based on those analyses.

Let's take a look at some examples.

We have here a rider that we'll refer to with the initials of JS, interacting with a prototype AI driver interaction system called Kitt (a bit of a small humor, the name is a play on the once popular TV series about a talking car).

01 – Kitt: Is your destination the Albertson's on Beach Boulevard?

02 – JS: Yes, it's the one that is near the In-and-Out Burger.

03 – Kitt: Okay, that Albertson's is about a block from the In-and-Out Burger. Let me know when you are ready to proceed to the Albertson's.

04 – JS: Let's go.

Notice that the AI system indicated the destination by stating the name of the place and the street that it was on. The AI could have instead merely recited the actual street address, but it has used a more culturally slang way to refer to the destination, giving it less of a robotic feel. This also though was based on the realization that there wasn't another Albertson's on Beach Boulevard, since if there was another one then the indication of the destination would have been ambiguous.

When JS responded, he provided what at first glance seems like an easy answer, he used the word "yes" to respond to the question.

But, he then added some additional information and the AI cannot just ignore the rest of the response. In this case, JS has apparently tried to clarify which Albertson's by saying that it is near another location, namely an In-and-Out Burger. I've just pointed out that there isn't another Albertson's on that street, and so you might wonder why JS would believe he has to clarify where the Albertson's is. It could be that he (falsely) thinks there's another one on Beach Boulevard, or that he just wanted to make sure that the AI wasn't confused about the location.

The AI echoes back to the rider that the Albertson's is indeed near to the In-and-Out Burger, which provides reassurance that both the driver and the rider are aiming for the same destination. If the AI had discovered that the In-and-Out Burger wasn't anywhere near the Albertson's, the dialogue would have gone in a different direction. Suppose there is a Ralph's on Beach Boulevard and it is near to the In-and-Out Burger, in which case, the AI would have asked JS whether he meant to say Ralph's rather than the Albertson's.

In any case, the AI next wanted to know whether JS was ready to proceed. This is a simple question but an important one. Just because JS has gotten into the car and closed the door, and confirmed the destination, does not mean that the AI can start ahead with the driving journey. Suppose JS is still getting settled into the passenger seat or otherwise is not ready to go. A simple question and a simple answer can ascertain whether to start or not.

Here's another example:

01 – JS: I need to get my wallet, which I left at home.

02 – Kitt: Are you saying that you want to first go home, before going to the Albertson's?

03 – JS: Yes, I need to go home first. I can't believe that I left my wallet. It seems like I keep forgetting to take it with me, probably because I bought this new pair of pants and the wallet doesn't fit well.

04 – Kitt: Confirming that you want to go home before going to

Albertson's. Changing direction now.

05 – JS: Thanks.

Notice that the rider has opted to alter a significant aspect of the driving journey. He has provided an indication that rather than directly going to Albertson's, he needs to be driven home first. There is some extraneous conversational snippet involved, in that he says he needs to get his wallet. Getting his wallet is not a clear-cut aspect of the driving journey and would be difficult to use as a means to determine that the destination needs to be changed. His indication that left it at home offers an implied aspect that he needs to go home. But, does he need to go home after visiting Albertson's or before visiting Albertson's. The likely guess is before, but the AI needs to get clarification from JS.

JS confirms that he wants to go to home first. He then goes off-topic in terms of the destination and provides an indication about his wallet. This snippet cannot be ignored by the AI, since there might be some other hidden instructions in it. After parsing his small soliloquy, the AI did not find anything pertinent to the driving task, and so opts to confirm that it will go ahead and head to his home first.

In the future, a more sophisticated social-behavioral computing capability would perhaps entertain the discussion about his wallet and his pants. A human driver would likely carry on such a discussion, perhaps lamenting how easy it is to forget a wallet or sympathizing with the difficultly of carrying the wallet in the new pants.

All of this conversation requires attention to the lexical, semantic, and syntactics aspects of human interaction. At the beginning of the two conversations, the AI took a leadership role in terms of shaping the direction of the conversation (doing so to affirm the desired destination). The human rider took over leadership in the second conversation, wanting to change the direction of the driving journey. There are predictable patterns of social action signatures (SAS) that exist in the driving journey task and topics arena, thus allowing the AI to provide a rather focused and on-target conversational assessment.

How far beyond the driving task should we have the AI go? Some would say that the AI should not venture far beyond the driving task. If it does so, it might mislead the rider into believing that the AI can do more than it can actually do. Most people that are using Alexa and Siri today are aware that it is not a fully capable form of natural language processing (NLP) in the sense that it does not comprehend in the same way that humans do. This is rather obvious after even just a few minutes of "conversing" with those NLP systems.

Critics concerned about the AI in self-driving cars are quite worried that the AI might appear to be more capable than it is, and that the human occupants will falsely believe that the AI can counsel them or otherwise do things it cannot do. As such, they want the AI to be good enough to carry on a limited conversation about the driving task, but not do so in a manner that suggests it has true human-like comprehension.

We can already predict that humans in AI self-driving cars are likely to anthropomorphize the AI system in the self-driving car. Given that humans spend a lot of time in their cars, it will be easy enough to start becoming comfortable with your autonomous driving chauffeur. Until the time at which the AI has progressed into Artificial General Intelligence (AGI), which is considered broad intelligence encompassing common sense and overall world knowledge, we should perhaps be cautious about how the AI converses about the driving journey and how it interacts with the human occupants. We want clarity of conversation without creating false impressions.

Hopefully, someday, it might be a truly wide-open socio-behavioral conversation.

CHAPTER 18
FLYING DEBRIS
AND
SELF-DRIVING CARS

CHAPTER 18

FLYING DEBRIS
AND SELF-DRIVING CARS

I was driving on the freeway the other day and up ahead of me the traffic started to do all sorts of dodging and weaving. Immediately, I suspected that there was likely some kind of debris that had caused drivers to enter into spasmatic moves of this nature. As I strained to see what was going on, I could just barely see white objects of maybe a half foot in length that were in the air and seemingly randomly bobbing around at the height of the car hoods and windshields. It was difficult to determine from my distance away as to whether the objects were inherently dangerous or not, but in a sense no matter what they were, it was still a dangerous circumstance due to the reaction by the other drivers. The act of the drivers swerving their cars had made the situation dicey and I was anticipating that some cars would ram into each other while playing this high-risk dodge game.

Upon reaching the point at which the objects were floating around, I was able to determine that they were actually pieces of mattress stuffing. Apparently, a mattress had fallen down onto the freeway, cars had hit and exploded open the mattress, which then disgorged the innards and the stuffing was being carried up into the air by the motion of the cars. Fortunately, having the mattress stuffing hit a car was not a serious matter per se, since it wouldn't do any direct damage. The biggest danger now was that the drivers were reacting madly and trying to keep from getting hit by the mattress fluff. They could have just driven straight ahead and not worried about hitting it. Instead, they were weaving as though it was poisonous and they didn't want to let it touch their cars.

Debris is always a potential issue for drivers as to whether to hit it or try to dodge it. There's the type of debris that sits on the actual roadway and driver's need to determine whether to hit it, or try to roll over it, or try to avoid it, all of which is tied to what damage the debris might cause to the underbelly of the car and whether or not the car will be able to continue unabated after striking the debris. If the roadway debris is someone's wool cap that flew out their car window and landed on the freeway, it's best to just run over it and continue along. If the back of a truck has dropped a couch onto the freeway, hitting it straight on is likely to damage the car and most drivers are going to do whatever they can to avoid hitting it.

Besides debris on the roadway, there's also airborne debris. This flying debris can originate as roadway debris, including the example earlier of a mattress that fell onto the freeway and then got split open after some cars hit it. The resulting spray of the mattress stuffing became an airborne mess. Car after car was making the material become increasing airborne and it was flitting back-and-forth across the lanes of traffic. In this case, the fluff was harmless, but the drivers were reacting to it anyway as though it was something that could harm their cars. That's a natural reaction for drivers. If they aren't sure of what it is, they are going to try and avoid it.

In fact, I'd assert that we have a natural aversion to anything that is flying towards us menacingly. As an example, about a month ago, I was on a highway and I saw what seemed like a large black plastic bag that was being hit repeatedly by cars ahead of me. It was flopping around and appeared to be empty. When my turn came to interact with the plastic bag, it swerved up towards my windshield. I admit that I flinched for a brief moment, even though logically I knew that it couldn't penetrate the windshield and would not be able to strike me. It's just a natural reaction we all have that if something aims toward your head, you are likely to flinch in an effort to try and avoid it.

There is roadway debris that can turn into flying debris, as exemplified by the mattress and also the black plastic bag, but that's not the only source of flying debris. Flying debris can appear seemingly out of nowhere and originate via other means.

A few years ago, I was driving along, minding my own business, when all of a sudden a golf ball struck my windshield. I had not even noticed beforehand that I was driving near a golf course, and so the loud smack upon my windshield was completely out-of-the-blue. The golf ball was moving so fast when it struck the windshield that I didn't even see it midflight beforehand. Once it hit, I then watched in horror as it cracked the windshield and then bounced away from my car. I was lucky it didn't penetrate through the windshield. In spite of the shock of the whole situation, I managed to continue driving forward and didn't swerve or otherwise react to the striking golf ball. Some drivers might have reacted and maybe gotten themselves into deeper trouble by swerving into other cars or possibly even driving off the highway and into a telephone pole.

On another occasion, I was driving under a freeway overpass, once again minding my own business, when all of a sudden a water balloon struck the windshield of my car. The water smeared across the windshield and for a brief heart-stopping moment I could not see out the windshield. Miraculously, my instinct took over and I turned on my windshield wipers to get the water out of my field of vision. This incident could have gone real bad, real quickly. Turns out there was some young thugs tossing water balloons onto cars, doing so from the overpass. They though it was pretty funny. You can imagine the kind of deathly car accidents that could have occurred. Not funny at all.

How do human drivers react to flying debris? Sometimes they swerve to try and avoid it. Or, they might hit the brakes in hopes of not striking the flying debris. Or, try to accelerate and get under it before it can land onto their cars. There are even some drivers that they themselves duck their heads and lose control of their cars, reacting as though the flying debris is going to physically harm them. Sometimes a driver just freezes up and slams into the flying debris. Overall, the circumstances and the nature of the driver are key factors in how the driver will react. Some drivers are cool and calm, others get flustered. Some situations involve debris that is relatively harmless, other situations involve debris that can do severe harm.

Via hindsight, you could say that the drivers that swerved to avoid the mattress fluff were wrong and perhaps "stupid" for having endangered other cars when they instead could have just driven straight into the stuffing. This is a hard call to make, though. At the moment of seeing the debris, you often have just a split second to decide what to do. And, your view of the debris might be different from other nearby drivers. Maybe you did not see that there was a mattress up ahead laying on the freeway, and so the white floating debris was an unknown item. You might not have been able to discern what the objects were, and so did the "safest" thing which seemed to be to try and avoid it.

There are a multitude of factors that come to play in dealing with flying debris, including:

- Perceived danger
- Actual danger
- Timing
- Traffic conditions
- Car capabilities
- Driving skill
- Driver awareness
- Occupants
- Pedestrians
- Weather conditions
- Roadway status
- Etc.

According to a study that looked at debris related incidents in the United States during the time period of 2011 to 2014, there were an estimated 200,000 car crashes that were attributable to debris situations. Of those 200,000 car crashes, there were about 39,000 people that were injured, and approximately 500 deaths. It's a staggering and sobering set of statistics. Furthermore, we don't know how many debris related incidents in total there were since these counts are only for those that led to a car crash. Suppose that for every debris related car crash there are 10x or maybe even 100x the number of incidents (but, who knows?), and so there could be possibly millions of debris related incidents that occur.

Often, the reaction to the debris is what leads to the car crashes and injuries. A car that swerves can end-up hitting another car, which then hits another car, and so on. The chain reaction that originates by the initial reaction to the debris can be the mainstay of how the car crashes arise. It's hard to say how many accidents could be avoided if the cars just drove through the debris and did not swerve or otherwise react. You could argue that maybe if we all agreed to always just drive straight through debris, we'd have lessened counts of car crashes that were debris related. It's hard though to be the driver of a car and realize that maybe if you are willing to get injured that it can save the lives of others and so be willing to not swerve your car. That's a tough pill to swallow.

What does this have to do with AI self-driving cars?

At the Cybernetic Self-Driving Car Institute, we are developing software to aid in the debris reaction of the AI systems.

We initially focused on debris sitting on the roadway and then have progressed into the flying debris aspects. AI self-driving cars that only deal with roadway debris are ill-prepared for flying debris.

That being said, some have said that they think an AI self-driving car should just ignore flying debris. The logic is that for a Level 5 self-driving car, which is a car that can be driven by the automation entirely and needs no human driver, there isn't a human driver that can get injured by flying debris so why worry about it. The viewpoint is that the AI can just keep driving forward and let the debris strike the car. This goes along with the aforementioned perspective that maybe we'd all be better off collectively if we didn't react to roadway debris.

Those that argue to ignore flying debris would assert that the flying debris isn't going to harm anything per se, and so just let it hit the car. Sure, it might crack the windshield, but so what, they say. This doesn't account for circumstances though that involve flying debris that can penetrate the windshield and then strike the humans inside the car. Just because there isn't a human driver doesn't mean that there aren't people inside the car. We still need to consider how to protect the human occupants.

The counter-argument is that the number of instances of flying debris that actually gets into the car compartment is very low, and so rather than trying to avoid the flying debris, it's safer overall to instruct all cars to just drive through it. One must also consider though that the flying debris could strike and break some of the sensors of the self-driving car, such as cameras mounted on the hood or a LIDAR system mounted on the top of the car. Harming the automation is certainly not the same as harming the humans, but at the same time keep in mind that if the automation gets harmed, it could mar the ability of the AI to drive the self-driving car, and a sudden loss of crucial sensors could lead to the self-driving car being unnavigable and lead to harm of humans both inside and outside of the vehicle.

The utopian self-driving car pundits would say that via V2V (vehicle-to-vehicle) communications of self-driving cars, we can ensure that swerving cars don't hit each other, and so it would be Okay to potentially swerve a car to avoid hitting debris. Using the exploding mattress example, presumably the first car that spots the mattress would electronically alert the other nearby cars. The other nearby cars would have their respective AI provide clearance to allow the detecting self-driving car to swerve. These self-driving cars would all then alert any upcoming self-driving cars to get out of the lane that contains the debris. The floating stuffing would be ranked as harmless by the self-driving cars and they would communicate to the other traffic that it's Okay to just run straight through the fluff.

The depicted utopian world is pretty nifty, but we're not going to have that world for many years to come. For a long time, we're going to have a mixture of both self-driving cars and human driven cars. There's not an easy way to alert the human drivers about the situation and so the V2V isn't going to get us the fully orchestrated and seamless dance of cars that the utopians envision.

The flying debris problem is multi-faceted and not so easy to solve. Is there a single piece of debris or are there multiple pieces of debris? Does the debris appear to be harmful or relatively harmless?

What is the predicted path of the flying debris? Is the flying debris being ricocheted off of other cars? How are other cars reacting? And so on.

The sensors of the AI self-driving car need to be detecting that the flying debris situations exists. Via the use of the cameras, radar, ultrasonic, LIDAR, and other sensors, the AI needs to interpret the incoming data and identify that there's a debris situation arising. In many cases, the debris itself won't be seen right away and instead the reaction of the other cars will be the clue that maybe debris is involved. You might recall that I noticed other cars dodging and weaving in the mattress instance, prior to my then seeing the white floating objects.

During sensor fusion, the AI is trying to piece together the telltale clues, which can be difficult to do because maybe the cameras don't yet see anything amiss, but perhaps the LIDAR has detected the flying debris. Each of the sensors has its own limits and capabilities. Some of the sensors can do detection at a greater distance than the others. The AI needs to update the virtual model of the surrounding environment and be preparing for a potential debris situation. As time clicks from split second to split second, the additional data flowing into the AI via the sensors will stepwise unveil what is happening in the driving situation.

The AI needs to be crafting an action plan of what to do. Stay in the same lane or switch lanes? Try to make a swerve or continue straight ahead? Apply the brakes? Add acceleration? These are all considered and must be placed into a sequence that can be applied. Time is crucial. Whatever sequence is developed must include the time to undertake the actions. Furthermore, once the sequence is started, the circumstances can change rapidly and so the action plan will need to be adjusted too. The AI emits commands to the controls of the self-driving car and must then pay attention to how the situation evolves.

Even getting the AI to do all of this for dealing with flying debris is only part of the solution to the problem. We also need to consider the human occupants in the car. Some say that the AI should just proceed to do whatever it needs to do and there's no need to alert the human occupants. They are just along for the ride.

But, this seems rather shortsighted. One could argue that the AI should warn the passengers that there is flying debris. It might give the human occupants a moment to prepare themselves for what might happen next, such as the swerving of the car and perhaps the impact by the debris. Others say that this is just going to scare the human occupants and since they aren't able to drive the car then it doesn't matter that they know in-advance what's going to happen. If anything, they might panic and tense up, perhaps getting further harmed or even needlessly harmed by the forewarning.

This takes us into the ethics aspects of AI self-driving cars. Do we want our self-driving cars to drive and not inform the human occupants about what is happening? This question is notably a one-way question and misses the other possible direction – suppose the human occupants are the first to spot the debris, and they want to alert the AI self-driving car that something is amiss, shouldn't they be able to do so? In other words, we have situations of the AI warning the occupants, and then the other situation of the occupants warning the AI.

What's even tougher in this matter is whether to have the humans be able to advise or direct the AI of the self-driving car. Suppose a human occupant yells out that there's debris and tells the AI to swerve to the left. Meanwhile, let's imagine that the AI has detected the debris and wants to drive straight through it. Should the AI proceed as it has planned, or should it do what the human says to do? You might say that the AI should interact with the human and reach an agreed solution, but realistically if the amount of time is split seconds then you're unlikely to have the luxury of a measured debate among people and machine.

We also need to consider the time aspects in the sense of stages, namely (1) pre-debris, (2) debris detection, (3) debris encounter, and (4) post-debris aspects.

In the HCI (Human Computer Interface), you could have a dialogue of the AI and the humans about what to do if there are any debris situations that might arise during a driving journey (this is during the pre-debris stage). For debris detection, the AI might alert the humans that debris has been detected and likewise might get input from the humans about the debris, depending upon the time allowed for such an interaction. During the debris encounter, the AI might be informing the humans about what is taking place. And, post-debris the AI might let them know what damage if any has occurred to the self-driving car, and likewise the humans might alert the AI to damages such as if the humans themselves have gotten injured (including indirectly perhaps due to whiplash by a swerving action of the car).

Conclusion

The flying debris problem is considered by many of the auto makers and tech firms as a so-called edge problem of self-driving cars. This means that it is not considered at the core of the self-driving car task. Little focus to-date is being put towards the flying debris issue. Nonetheless, per driving stats, it is well-known that debris is an issue for cars on the roadway and we'll need to ultimately figure out how to have AI self-driving cars that can properly take action in the face of debris, whether it's on the roadway or flying, or both. This also includes ensuring that there is appropriate interaction with the human occupants of the self-driving car. They do indeed matter.

Lance B. Eliot

CHAPTER 19

CITIZEN AI

FOR SELF-DRIVING CARS

CHAPTER 19

CITIZEN AI

FOR SELF-DRIVING CARS

Have you ever heard of the phrase "citizen scientists"?

The phrases first entered into our lexicon in the mid-1990's, and generally refers to the notion that ordinary everyday people can potentially contribute to the work of science, in spite of the fact that they aren't professional scientists. We usually have some disdain for amateurs or non-professionals that try to enter into a professional realm, and we tend to denigrate whatever kind of contribution they might try to make. What do they know about real science, some ask. They are prone to fake science, some accuse.

The word "citizen" in this context is meant to suggest the lay public. In more recent times, we've generally seen that the word "crowd" has perhaps overtaken the now quainter use of the word citizen. We have crowd sourcing, and many refer nowadays to the "wisdom of the crowd" whenever we see lots of people band together on social media such as Facebook or Twitter. The crowd has become the plural version of the citizen, suggesting that with the crowd we have large numbers of contributors, while the word "citizen" can refer to just one person or possibly many such citizens contributing either individually or possibly banding together as a collective.

Using that same idea of the public contributing toward something that is outside of their expertise, we will soon be entering into an era of Citizen AI. In other words, we should begin to anticipate that everyday folks will want to contribute to the AI field. There will be

241

those within AI that will certainly be skeptical about this notion. Only AI developers can develop AI, they will say. AI researchers will be horrified to see non-AI versed lay people that profess to offer new innovations in AI. Similar to those skeptics of citizen science, we're likely to have skeptics of Citizen AI.

Now, let's be clear that there's a basis for being skeptical of both citizen science and citizen AI. For true science, we expect that scientists will be careful in their work, they will abide by proven scientific methods, they will document carefully their work, they will refrain from making unsupported conclusions, and so on. They are trained in these scientific approaches and can be held accountable within the community of scientists. In contrast, citizen scientists can presumably do whatever they want and make whatever outlandish claims they might wish to make. As such, one certainly should be skeptical and cautious when considering work or outcomes reported by citizen scientists.

For AI, we can say the same. AI developers are supposed to be versed in the techniques and approaches of AI. They should be careful about how they develop AI systems. They should be doing proper testing of their AI systems. They should be mindful of making outlandish claims. Unfortunately, there's not quite the same overall code of conduct for AI as there are for scientists overall. This means that there are a number of AI developers and AI researchers that aren't as closely held accountable for their claims. This makes it easier for citizen AI participants to enter into the fray. They can point to professional AI developers and researchers and point out potential guffaws and unsupported claims, and therefore argue that they should have similar latitude.

Please be aware that the phrase "Citizen AI" is not yet standardized and there are other uses associated with the meaning of the phrase. Some for example assert that it means that AI needs to stand-up for the citizenry. AI developers and researchers are supposed to consider the societal implications of the AI that they are bringing forth into the world. These AI innovations need to show their citizenry and the AI developers need to indicate how society and its citizens will benefit by the AI and not be harmed by the AI. I somewhat doubt that this meaning is going to take hold per se, since it doesn't seem aligned with the Citizen Science meaning and so ends-up being more confusing than clarifying. Time will tell.

Back to then the meaning here of Citizen AI, which is that we are gradually going to have members of the general public that will be aiding the advancement of AI.

Ridiculous, you might say. Not so much, some retort. With recent advances in AI tools, we are seeing the arcane and highly complex aspects of AI coming further and further outside of the inner sanctum of obscure research labs. Conventional software developers are now routinely making use of AI by connecting with online AI systems and using Application Programming Interfaces (API's) to have their traditional non-AI code leverage AI capabilities such as natural language processing, image analyses, artificial neural networks, and the like. It won't be much longer before these AI tools are so easy to use that just about anyone can use them, ergo, the emergence of Citizen AI.

What does this have to do with AI self-driving cars?

At the Cybernetic Self-Driving Car Institute, we are anticipating that everyday people will ultimately want to alter, add, or in some manner impact the AI that is driving their self-driving cars.

This comes as a shock to many of the auto makers and tech firms that are creating the AI for self-driving cars. For most of them, they are assuming that the AI on the self-driving cars will be a completely closed and locked system. Nobody, but nobody, gets into those systems, other than the auto maker or tech firm that made the system. This certainly makes sense at first glance, since we are talking about AI that controls a car, and therefore involves life-and-death circumstances.

Just imagine if you let a Citizen AI that opts to make a change to the sensors of a self-driving car and then, oops, the sensor interprets images of cars to be images of flowers. Some crazy minded goofball action like this would make the self-driving car do bad things. In some cases, the citizen AI might be doing something of an innocent nature and inadvertently mucking up the AI of the self-driving car, while in other cases it might be someone with a dastardly intent and they are purposely trying to make a self-driving car do terrible acts.

So, let's for the moment say that allowing any kind of Citizen AI for self-driving cars is nonsensical and we'll go along with the prevailing wisdom that the AI for the self-driving car is closed and locked. Well, there will always be those car hobbyists that will try to find a means around the closed and locked system. They will tinker and try. They will look for any small crack to pry open. You've likely heard of jail breaking your smart phone, and you can anticipate that some Citizen AI car hobbyists will be seeking to do the same to the AI of self-driving cars.

One way to try and curtail those activities would be to make it a crime to do so. The government could put in place laws that make it illegal to try and reverse engineer or otherwise crack open the AI of self-driving cars. This would certainly reduce the number of Citizen AI contributors regarding self-driving cars, but probably not get it to zero since there will still be those lawbreakers that are willing to go against the law for what they believe is right.

Indeed, I would anticipate that we'll have some Citizen AI contributors that would say that by making it illegal to try and pry into the AI of self-driving cars that the government is putting the people at risk of faulty AI made by the auto makers or tech firms. And, if you buy into conspiracy theories, these Citizen AIers might argue that we could end-up with the AI of the self-driving cars taking over our self-driving cars, and without us citizens being able to get inside to stop it, we'd be at the mercy of this AI gone mad.

Though this last doomsday scenario is probably a better movie script than reality, the aspect that we are going to have only and always closed and locked AI for our AI self-driving cars seems rather suspect. We might be able to find some acceptable middle ground. Suppose that instead of the impenetrable barrier goal, we instead provide ways in which the AI of the self-driving can be adjusted, though in relatively controllable ways.

You can already bet that there are going to be third-party developers that will want to tie into the AI of the self-driving car. Just like there are add-on's for our computers and our smart phones, there are bound to be a plethora of add-on's that will emerge for self-driving cars. Currently, there are about 200 million conventional cars in the United States alone, and so if we are someday going to have that same number or more of AI self-driving cars, it's a pretty tempting market for third-parties that want to make big bucks by supplementing whatever the auto maker has provided for the AI of your self-driving car.

What kinds of add-on's would make sense?

Suppose that for the sensors of your self-driving car that the version of AI provided by the auto maker is adequate for detecting snow generally, but then a third-party developer enhances that capability for snow found in Colorado Springs in particular (note that Colorado Springs gets about 70 inches of snow per year). The add-on takes into account the specific geography of Colorado Springs and aids the conventional snow-analysis routines that come with your standard AI self-driving car. Would you be Okay with this add-on?

Now, you wouldn't presumably proceed with the add-on unless you knew that it was well tested and able to work properly. Including this add-on would possibly confuse the standard AI snow-analysis routines if it was improperly coded, and so there is a downside to adding such an add-on. Presumably, the auto maker of the AI could have a certification program, whereby the third-party add-on needs to demonstrate that it works as intended and that it doesn't work improperly. Just in case some people opted to get uncertified add-on's, the auto maker might even make the AI of the self-driving car closed and locked to anything but properly certified add-on's.

If you have now become somewhat convinced that maybe the AI of the self-driving car should allow for being semi-open, in this case for these third-party certified and approved add-on's, you might then be ready to accept the idea of Citizen AI for the AI of the self-driving car. Now, I realize that the third-party add-on would likely have been developed by professional AI developers, and so it is not really considered a Citizen AI effort. But, it takes us one step closer to allowing for Citizen AI efforts for the AI of self-driving cars.

There are parts of the AI of the AI self-driving car that we likely would consider sacrosanct and not allow any kind of add-on's or modifications by anyone other than the auto maker or tech firm. The core aspects of sensor analysis for the radar, cameras, LIDAR, ultrasonic are areas we'd most likely want to keep pure. The same could be said of the sensor fusion, and the virtual world model of the AI for the self-driving car, and the action plans, and the controls activation.

Where we might see allowance for Citizen AI would be at the outer areas of these cores elements. Though this might be allowed, in the end, the rest of the AI of the self-driving car would still be the overall controlling element of the driving of the car. In other words, no added element would be able to avoid being within the control of the bona fide AI. If the bona fide AI opted to nullify or momentarily turn-off the add-on, it could do so as needed. This would help to prevent some accidental rouge add-on from making chaos.

For those of you with an eye toward computer security, you might be wondering whether it is sensible to allow any kind of openings into the AI of the AI self-driving car. We are likely to already have hackers that will be virulently trying to find ways into the AI, hoping that they can take over the control of the self-driving car or maybe have an entire fleet of cars do their bidding. Admittedly, providing an opening for their efforts by having an opening for add-on's does up the ante on the computer security aspects. But, an argument could be made that it actually forces the auto makers and tech firms to be on their toes about the computer security of the self-driving car.

There's another twist to this topic that at first might not seem apparent. We have car hobbyists today that will take apart cars and remake them into their own image, so to speak, by deciding to add new components or change up components. In theory, such cars are supposed to be street-legal if they are intended to be used on our public roads. Suppose that a devoted car hobbyist opts to take apart a purchased AI self-driving car and remake it. Maybe they even discard the AI software and write their own.

If you saw an AI self-driving car driving on the roadways, how would you know that it is a legitimate one that came from a bona fide auto maker or tech firm, versus that it was a hot rod version that some car hobbyist put together? Of course, federal and state regulations are intended to hamper those that would want to do such a thing, by legally forcing them to make sure the self-driving car was street legal, but the answer to the question is that you would not have any means particularly of knowing that the self-driving car next to you is fully legal.

Let's take another angle on the same notion. Currently, it is anticipated that the early days of self-driving cars will consist of cars that were made purposely to be a self-driving car. In essence, the car is likely not going to be a purely conventional car that just so happens to have some added sensory equipment bolted onto it. Eventually, though, many believe that we will have "converter kits" that allow you to turn a somewhat conventional car into an AI self-driving car. Once we get there, you can pretty much bet that then we'll for sure have Citizen AI that opts to tinker with those converter kits.

This discussion on Citizen AI for AI self-driving cars is a somewhat futuristic look at where things are going. We don't yet have sufficient numbers of AI self-driving cars on the roadway to see how this is going to play out. We've not yet seen Citizen AI come to bear on for example Tesla's, which though they aren't yet true AI self-driving cars (they are below the Level 5), and so we haven't seen this happening to-date.

Nonetheless, it does seem like a strong possibility that once we get enough AI self-driving cars on our roadways we are going to have Citizen AI for AI self-driving cars. Depending upon your perspective on the matter, you are either eager to see that day arrive, or you are dreading that day and pledge that should that day occur you will never ride in an AI self-driving car again. Or does that make you a Luddite?

Lance B. Eliot

APPENDIX

APPENDIX A
TEACHING WITH THIS MATERIAL

The material in this book can be readily used either as a supplemental to other content for a class, or it can also be used as a core set of textbook material for a specialized class. Classes where this material is most likely used include any classes at the college or university level that want to augment the class by offering thought provoking and educational essays about AI and self-driving cars.

In particular, here are some aspects for class use:

o   Computer Science. Studying AI, autonomous vehicles, etc.

o   Business. Exploring technology and it adoption for business.

o   Sociology. Sociological views on the adoption and advancement of technology.

Specialized classes at the undergraduate and graduate level can also make use of this material.

For each chapter, consider whether you think the chapter provides material relevant to your course topic. There is plenty of opportunity to get the students thinking about the topic and force them to decide whether they agree or disagree with the points offered and positions taken. I would also encourage you to have the students do additional research beyond the chapter material presented (I provide next some suggested assignments they can do).

RESEARCH ASSIGNMENTS ON THESE TOPICS

Your students can find background material on these topics, doing so in various business and technical publications. I list below the top ranked AI related journals. For business publications, I would suggest the usual culprits such as the Harvard Business Review, Forbes, Fortune, WSJ, and the like.

Here are some suggestions of homework or projects that you could assign to students:

a) <u>Assignment for foundational AI research topic</u>: Research and prepare a paper and a presentation on a specific aspect of Deep AI, Machine Learning, ANN, etc. The paper should cite at least 3 reputable sources. Compare and contrast to what has been stated in this book.

b) <u>Assignment for the Self-Driving Car topic</u>: Research and prepare a paper and Self-Driving Cars. Cite at least 3 reputable sources and analyze the characterizations. Compare and contrast to what has been stated in this book.

c) <u>Assignment for a Business topic</u>: Research and prepare a paper and a presentation on businesses and advanced technology. What is hot, and what is not? Cite at least 3 reputable sources. Compare and contrast to the depictions in this book.

d) <u>Assignment to do a Startup:</u> Have the students prepare a paper about how they might startup a business in this realm. They must submit a sound Business Plan for the startup. They could also be asked to present their Business Plan and so should also have a presentation deck to coincide with it.

You can certainly adjust the aforementioned assignments to fit to your particular needs and the class structure. You'll notice that I ask for 3 reputable cited sources for the paper writing based assignments. I usually steer students toward "reputable" publications, since otherwise they will cite some oddball source that has no credentials other than that they happened to write something and post it onto the Internet. You can define "reputable" in whatever way you prefer, for example some faculty think Wikipedia is not reputable while others believe it is reputable and allow students to cite it.

The reason that I usually ask for at least 3 citations is that if the student only does one or two citations they usually settle on whatever they happened to find the fastest. By requiring three citations, it usually seems to force them to look around, explore, and end-up probably finding five or more, and then whittling it down to 3 that they will actually use.

I have not specified the length of their papers, and leave that to you to tell the students what you prefer. For each of those assignments, you could end-up with a short one to two pager, or you could do a dissertation length paper. Base the length on whatever best fits for your class, and the credit amount of the assignment within the context of the other grading metrics you'll be using for the class.

I mention in the assignments that they are to do a paper and prepare a presentation. I usually try to get students to present their work. This is a good practice for what they will do in the business world. Most of the time, they will be required to prepare an analysis and present it. If you don't have the class time or inclination to have the students present, then you can of course cut out the aspect of them putting together a presentation.

If you want to point students toward highly ranked journals in AI, here's a list of the top journals as reported by *various citation counts sources* (this list changes year to year):

- o Communications of the ACM
- o Artificial Intelligence
- o Cognitive Science
- o IEEE Transactions on Pattern Analysis and Machine Intelligence
- o Foundations and Trends in Machine Learning
- o Journal of Memory and Language
- o Cognitive Psychology
- o Neural Networks
- o IEEE Transactions on Neural Networks and Learning Systems
- o IEEE Intelligent Systems
- o Knowledge-based Systems

GUIDE TO USING THE CHAPTERS

For each of the chapters, I provide next some various ways to use the chapter material. You can assign the tasks as individual homework assignments, or the tasks can be used with team projects for the class. You can easily layout a series of assignments, such as indicating that the students are to do item "a" below for say Chapter 1, then "b" for the next chapter of the book, and so on.

a) What is the main point of the chapter and describe in your own words the significance of the topic,

b) Identify at least two aspects in the chapter that you agree with, and support your concurrence by providing at least one other outside researched item as support; make sure to explain your basis for disagreeing with the aspects,

c) Identify at least two aspects in the chapter that you disagree with, and support your disagreement by providing at least one other outside researched item as support; make sure to explain your basis for disagreeing with the aspects,

d) Find an aspect that was not covered in the chapter, doing so by conducting outside research, and then explain how that aspect ties into the chapter and what significance it brings to the topic,

e) Interview a specialist in industry about the topic of the chapter, collect from them their thoughts and opinions, and readdress the chapter by citing your source and how they compared and contrasted to the material,

f) Interview a relevant academic professor or researcher in a college or university about the topic of the chapter, collect from them their thoughts and opinions, and readdress the chapter by citing your source and how they compared and contrasted to the material,

g) Try to update a chapter by finding out the latest on the topic, and ascertain whether the issue or topic has now been solved or whether it is still being addressed, explain what you come up with.

The above are all ways in which you can get the students of your class involved in considering the material of a given chapter. You could mix things up by having one of those above assignments per each week, covering the chapters over the course of the semester or quarter.

As a reminder, here are the chapters of the book and you can select whichever chapters you find most valued for your particular class:

Advances in AI and Autonomous Vehicles:
Cybernetic Self-Driving Cars

Practical Advances in Artificial Intelligence (AI)
and Machine Learning
by
Dr. Lance B. Eliot, MBA, PhD

This title is available via Amazon and other book sellers

Companion Book By This Author

Self-Driving Cars:
"The Mother of All AI Projects"

by Dr. Lance B. Eliot, MBA, PhD

This title is available via Amazon and other book sellers

This title is available via Amazon and other book sellers

<u>Companion Book By This Author</u>

***New Advances in AI Autonomous
Driverless Cars Self-Driving Cars***

by Dr. Lance B. Eliot, MBA, PhD

<u>Chapter Title</u>

This title is available via Amazon and other book sellers

This title is available via Amazon and other book sellers

Lance B. Eliot

<u>Companion Book By This Author</u>

Autonomous Vehicle Driverless Self-Driving Cars and Artificial Intelligence

by Dr. Lance B. Eliot, MBA, PhD

<u>Chapter Title</u>

This title is available via Amazon and other book sellers

ABOUT THE AUTHOR

Dr. Lance B. Eliot, MBA, PhD is the CEO of Techbruim, Inc. and Executive Director of the Cybernetic Self-Driving Car Institute, and has over twenty years of industry experience including serving as a corporate officer in a billion dollar firm and was a partner in a major executive services firm. He is also a serial entrepreneur having founded, ran, and sold several high-tech related businesses. He previously hosted the popular radio show *Technotrends* that was also available on American Airlines flights via their in-flight audio program. Author or co-author of a dozen books and over 400 articles, he has made appearances on CNN, and has been a frequent speaker at industry conferences.

A former professor at the University of Southern California (USC), he founded and led an innovative research lab on Artificial Intelligence in Business. Known as the "AI Insider" his writings on AI advances and trends has been widely read and cited. He also previously served on the faculty of the University of California Los Angeles (UCLA), and was a visiting professor at other major universities. He was elected to the International Board of the Society for Information Management (SIM), a prestigious association of over 3,000 high-tech executives worldwide.

He has performed extensive community service, including serving as Senior Science Adviser to the Vice Chair of the Congressional Committee on Science & Technology. He has served on the Board of the OC Science & Engineering Fair (OCSEF), where he is also has been a Grand Sweepstakes judge, and likewise served as a judge for the Intel International SEF (ISEF). He served as the Vice Chair of the Association for Computing Machinery (ACM) Chapter, a prestigious association of computer scientists. Dr. Eliot has been a shark tank judge for the USC Mark Stevens Center for Innovation on start-up pitch competitions, and served as a mentor for several incubators and accelerators in Silicon Valley and Silicon Beach. He served on several Boards and Committees at USC, including having served on the Marshall Alumni Association (MAA) Board in Southern California.

Dr. Eliot holds a PhD from USC, MBA, and Bachelor's in Computer Science, and earned the CDP, CCP, CSP, CDE, and CISA certifications. Born and raised in Southern California, and having traveled and lived internationally, he enjoys scuba diving, surfing, and sailing.

ADDENDUM

Transformative AI Driverless Self-Driving Cars

Practical Advances in Artificial Intelligence (AI) and Machine Learning

By

Dr. Lance B. Eliot, MBA, PhD

———

For supplemental materials of this book, visit:

www.lance-blog.com

For special orders of this book, contact:

LBE Press Publishing

Email: LBE.Press.Publishing@gmail.com

www.ingramcontent.com/pod-product-compliance
Lightning Source LLC
Chambersburg PA
CBHW051226050326
40689CB00007B/818